Buddy Oliver

LET'S COOK

Photography DAVID LOFTUS & PAUL STUART

appetite
by RANDOM HOUSE

CONTENTS

Breakfast sandwich
Peasto pasta
Mini quiches
Rocky road
Grilled chicken lollipops
Quick and easy pizzas
All-purpose tomato sauce

BUDD
DEN

HELLO, IT'S BUDDY!

First of all, I want to say that I'm happy you're here! Cooking is one of my all-time favorite things to do. It's really fun, and a great skill to learn. Once you know the basics, you can give most recipes a try, or even have a go at making your own! It doesn't always go as planned, but that doesn't matter. I like to cook for my brother and sisters, but I also cook for my friends sometimes. If you make something exactly how *you* like it, you'll want to eat it, and it's good not always having to rely on grown-ups!

One of the first things I ever cooked was scrambled eggs – they were really tasty, and are actually so simple once you know how. It made me want to see what else I could do. I learned to make things like chopped salads from helping Mum or Dad in the kitchen, and even started to make pizza and bread. The more I learned, the more I wanted to explore.

This book is full of the things I love to cook and eat. It's not fancy or hard to follow, it's just simple food done nicely (I hope you agree). My absolute favorite recipe is the Easy spaghetti and meatballs because it's fun to make and tastes so good. I'm a big pasta fan, so there's a whole chapter of easy pastas in the book.

My family favorites chapter is probably the one I cook from the most. It's all the things I like to eat at home, and can now make myself – things like fajitas, fish cakes, Bolognese and fish stick sandwiches. I've also got some tasty breakfast and brunch recipes – brunch is for when you've got a bit more time to enjoy eating on the weekends, and that's when I tend to have more time to cook, too. I've included some after-school bites – things you can eat quickly when you get home. I'm always hungry then! And I also love to make cakes and desserts because they're sweet and delicious, but I do sometimes make a bit of a mess!

I've had so much fun in the last few years creating *Cooking Buddies* and sharing my recipes. Making a TV show was epic – it was really fun to learn some cool new skills from other kids, but also to teach them dishes that they can share with their friends. You can watch lots of great how-to and recipe videos on my *Cooking Buddies* YouTube channel. Have fun!

Together

A WORD FROM DAD

There's something so powerful about being able to cook. You could even call it a superpower – one that grants you real freedom when it comes to what you want to eat. I'll let you in on a little secret: the key to learning to cook is being curious and having the confidence to give it a try. Not everything will work out perfectly – and that's okay. Sometimes, when things don't go as planned, you might still end up with something delicious, just not what you were expecting!

Buddy and his brother and sisters have all grown up around food, but Buddy, out of all of them, has always found it effortlessly exciting – a real adventure. He's been my shadow in the kitchen since he was tiny, and the skills he's gained are unreal. I'm super proud of this book and the effort he's put into building up *Cooking Buddies* over the last few years.

Now, even if this is your first cookbook, you're never too young to start making incredible things, digging in, and having a laugh and enjoying yourself along the way. Think of a recipe a bit like a treasure map – something that gets you from A to B – with a prize (a tasty bite to eat!) at the end. It really is super fun. I was just eight years old when I properly started to cook, and I haven't looked back since.

So, guys, what are you waiting for? Put colored stickies on the pages of the things you want to make, and ask a grown-up if you can get the ingredients and give them a try. Get those adults working for you ;)

NOW GROWN-UPS...

Please believe me when I say you will never regret encouraging your children to learn how to cook. I'm not talking about cheffy recipes with complicated techniques, just good, simple, nutritious, fun food that will help fuel your kids with the right stuff. Trust me, knowing how to make a bowl of pasta or a simple soup are skills that will set them up for life.

There's something incredibly powerful about giving kids the freedom to make their own decisions about the food they eat. Having a bit of control over the shopping and the cooking means that they can make it in the way they like it, which will ultimately help us out on our quest to get them eating well. Lots of parents are lost when it comes to the quirks of feeding their kids (me included!), so it's always worth trying a new approach.

Knowing how to cook is one of the most important gifts you can give a child, and if you want to brush up on your own kitchen skills, too, why not pick a new recipe and make it together. It's wonderful to see the sense of pride when a child realizes that they can make a valuable contribution to family mealtimes.

On the pages that follow, you'll find a lovely bunch of tested and trusted recipes for you and your family to use week in, week out. There's a mixture of cool and contemporary dishes, a whole collection of family favorites (with plenty of the good stuff built in!), as well as after-school bites and some much-loved sweet treats. Buddy has also included a chapter called "Skills for life," which is full of basic recipes you can work your way through to really check off those easy-but-important everyday kitchen skills. And remember, don't worry if you don't have the exact ingredients listed on each page, you can be flexible with the type or variety, or swap things in and out as you please – for things like oil, cheese or seasonal produce, choose your favorite or just use what you have on hand.

I hope that this book will help your kids fall in love with a whole rainbow of beautiful ingredients and flavors.

Big love, Jamie O xxx

BREAKFAST AND BRUNCH

Serves 1 Minutes 9

Breakfast sandwich

With a baked bean dipper

You need

1 oz Cheddar cheese

2 slices of bread

1 large egg

optional: 2 slices of smoked bacon

⅓ cup baked beans or homemade beans (see page 122)

1. Switch your toastie maker or panini press on to warm up.
2. Grate the cheese over one of the slices of bread.
3. Push and squash the bread down to create a pocket in the center, then carefully crack in the egg and top with the second piece of bread.
4. Stretch out the bacon slices slightly (if using), then carefully wrap them around the outside of the bread.
5. Carefully transfer to the toastie maker or panini press, then clamp the lid down and toast for 5 minutes, or until golden and crisp.
6. Heat the beans in a small pan or in the microwave and serve alongside.

> **“If using regular baked beans here, spice them up with a shake of Worcestershire sauce and a dash or two of Tabasco – so good!”**

Plus resting

Egg tortilla wrap

With salsa and smashed avo

You need

⅔ cup whole wheat flour

olive oil

1 large ripe tomato (about 5 oz)

3 scallions

1 small red bell pepper

½ a bunch of basil (about ½ oz)

red wine vinegar

½ a ripe avocado

4 medium eggs

1 oz Cheddar cheese

Time-saver alert!

Swap in store-bought tortillas to speed this one right up!

1. Add the flour to a mixing bowl, stir in a pinch of sea salt, then make a well in the middle. Pour in ¼ cup of warm water and 1 tablespoon of olive oil, then use a fork to bring in the flour from the outside to form a dough – when the dough starts to come together, dust your hands with flour and pat it into a ball.
2. Knead on a lightly-floured surface for a few minutes, or until smooth and elastic. Cover and let rest for 30 minutes.
3. Seed the tomato and roughly chop three-quarters of it, trim and thinly slice 2 scallions and seed and finely chop the pepper, then scrape into a bowl. Tear in the basil leaves, drizzle with 1 teaspoon each of olive oil and red wine vinegar, then toss together and season to taste.
4. Peel and pit the avocado (if needed), scoop into a bowl, then mash with a fork. Trim the remaining scallion and finely dice with the remaining tomato, then stir into the avocado.
5. Split the dough in half, roll each piece into a ball, then use a rolling pin to roll each one out into a circle roughly 9 inches in diameter.
6. Place a 10-inch non-stick frying pan over medium heat and, one at a time, cook the tortillas for 1 minute on each side, then remove.
7. Beat the eggs in a bowl with a pinch each of salt and black pepper.
8. Drizzle 1 teaspoon of olive oil into the pan, then carefully wipe it around with a ball of paper towels. Pour in half the egg, tilt the pan to coat, place a cooked tortilla on top and cook for 1 minute, then flip.
9. Finely grate on half the cheese, let melt for 30 seconds to 1 minute, then carefully slide onto a plate.
10. Spread half the smashed avo onto the tortilla, top with half the tomato salsa, then roll up. Repeat with the remaining ingredients.

Portions **12** Minutes **15**

Chocolatey oatmeal

With yogurt and fresh fruit

You need

1¾ cups slivered almonds

8 Medjool dates

5 cups old-fashioned rolled oats

2 teaspoons ground cinnamon

3 heaping tablespoons high-quality unsweetened cocoa powder

1 orange

To serve (per portion)

¾ cup milk

1 generous tablespoon Greek or plain yogurt

¼ to ½ cup fresh fruit, such as orange segments, blueberries, raspberries, blackberries, sliced banana or grated apple and pear

1 Toast the almonds in a dry non-stick frying pan over medium heat and toast until golden, stirring regularly, then transfer to a food processor.

2 Pit the dates, then tear the flesh into the processor. Add half the oats, the cinnamon and the cocoa powder.

3 Finely grate in the orange zest and pulse until fine, then add the mixture to a bowl with the remaining oats and stir to combine. Transfer to an airtight jar, ready to use – it'll keep for a couple of weeks (or more!).

4 To make a bowl of oatmeal, simply put ½ cup of the mixture into a saucepan with the milk and heat over medium-low heat for 3 minutes, or until it's the consistency that you like, stirring regularly and adding splashes of water to loosen, if needed.

5 Top each bowlful with a spoonful of yogurt and your favorite seasonal fruit. Just remember, if you cook multiple portions at once, simply increase the cooking time slightly.

Did you know?

Using high-quality unsweetened cocoa powder here instead of regular chocolate will give you that much-loved chocolatey goodness, but it's nutritious for you, too – bonus!

Serves 2 Minutes 5

Rainbow smoothies

With banana, milk and almonds or oats

You need

1 banana

3 tablespoons almond flour or ¼ cup old-fashioned rolled oats

1 cup milk

2 handfuls of frozen mango, frozen mixed berries, frozen cherries or baby spinach (or a mixture)

1. Peel and slice the banana (ideally you want to use a frozen banana, so try to remember to do this the day before and pop it in the freezer).
2. Add the banana, almond flour or oats and milk to a blender. Add your chosen fruits and veg, secure the lid and blitz until smooth.
3. Pour into glasses and serve.

Overripe bananas?

Peel and roughly chop any bananas that are soft and dark brown, squeeze on a little lime juice (this stops the bananas going brown), then pop them into a reusable freezer bag in a single layer to prevent them from sticking together and freeze until solid.

Poached eggs

You need

2 large eggs

1 English muffin

unsalted butter

> “I cook these every week. So easy and really, really tasty.”

1 Add enough water to a large saucepan to fill it halfway, add a pinch of sea salt, then bring to a gentle simmer over medium heat.

2 Crack one of the eggs into a cup, then gently pour it into the water in one go, and repeat – the eggs will start to cook right away, and don't worry if the edges look a bit wispy.

3 For a really soft poached egg, cook for about 2 minutes, and for a soft-to-firm egg, cook for 4 minutes – these times may vary slightly depending on the size of the pan you use.

4 To check whether the eggs are done, lift one out of the water with a slotted spoon and give it a gentle poke with a teaspoon. If it feels too soft, carefully pop it back in for another minute or two. When you're happy, remove the eggs and place on paper towels to dry off.

5 Halve the muffin and toast until golden, then spread lightly with butter and spoon a poached egg onto each half.

Scrambled eggs

You need

2 eggs

optional: soft herbs such as Italian parsley or chives

unsalted butter

1 slice of bread

1 Crack the eggs into a bowl, season with a pinch each of sea salt and black pepper, and beat together well.

2 Pick, finely chop and add the herbs (if using). Heat about ½ tablespoon of butter in a non-stick frying pan over low heat, and once melted, pour in the eggs.

3 Stir slowly with a rubber or silicone spatula until the eggs look silky and slightly underdone, then remove from the heat.

4 Toast and butter the bread, then place on a plate and spoon on the scrambled eggs.

Fried eggs

Serves 1 Minutes 8

You need

olive oil

2 eggs

1 slice of bread

unsalted butter

1 Drizzle 2 tablespoons of olive oil into a large non-stick frying pan over medium-low heat.

2 Carefully crack the eggs into the pan, and when they turn white, tilt the pan and carefully spoon some of the hot oil over the eggs – this will help them to cook through evenly.

3 Use a slotted spatula to carefully transfer the eggs to paper towels to drain, gently patting them dry.

4 Toast and butter the bread, place on a plate and top with the fried eggs.

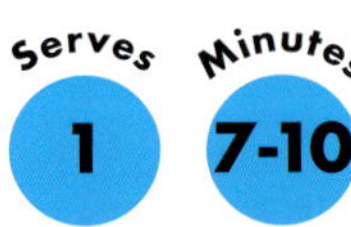

Boiled eggs

You need

2 large eggs

1 slice of bread

unsalted butter

1 Bring a small saucepan of salted water to a boil over high heat.

2 Using a spoon, dip the eggs in and out of the water a few times (this helps prevent them from shocking and cracking), then slowly lower them into the pan.

3 Cook for the following times, depending on how you like your eggs: 5 minutes for runny or 7½ minutes for semi-firm (if you want to make a hard-boiled egg, cook for 10 minutes), then transfer to egg cups.

4 Toast and butter the bread, then cut into soldiers. Lightly tap and remove the top of the egg and start dunking.

Savory breakfast muffins

With a crunchy seed topping

You need

3 oz Cheddar or Parmesan cheese

4 cups baby spinach (about 4 oz)

optional: 1 red chili

2 scallions

¾ cup milk

¼ cup olive oil

2 large eggs

2½ cups whole wheat flour

3¾ teaspoons baking powder

½ teaspoon salt

2 oz feta cheese

2 tablespoons mixed seeds, such as sesame, sunflower, pumpkin and poppy

1 Preheat the oven to 350°F, and line a 12-cup muffin tin with paper liners.

2 Grate the Cheddar or Parmesan and place in a mixing bowl. Finely chop half the spinach and roughly chop the rest, then add to the bowl.

3 Seed and finely chop the chili (if using), trim and finely chop the scallions, then add to the bowl.

4 Pour the milk and olive oil into a separate mixing bowl, crack in the eggs and mix well. Fold in the flour, baking powder and salt and all the ingredients from the other bowl.

5 Divide half the batter among the prepared muffin cups, then crumble on the feta, dividing evenly, and spoon in the rest of the batter. Sprinkle with your chosen seeds, then bake for 20 minutes, or until golden and cooked through – if you poke a skewer into the middle, it should come out clean.

6 Let cool slightly in the pan, then transfer to a wire rack – delicious served warm or cold.

Bonus flavor

If you've got any leftover ham, roast chicken or different cheeses, or even things like olives and tomatoes, these can all be chopped up and added to this recipe – it's super-flexible!

Serves **2** Minutes **15**

Eggy bread

With raspberry ripple yogurt and nut butter

You need

2 large eggs

2 tablespoons milk

olive oil

2 x ½-inch slices of bread

2 teaspoons of your favorite nut butter

generous 1 cup raspberries

2 generous tablespoons plain yogurt

optional: 1 sprig of mint

runny honey, to serve

1 Crack the eggs into a shallow bowl, add the milk, then whisk together.

2 Place a large non-stick frying pan over medium heat. Drizzle ½ tablespoon of olive oil into the pan and carefully swirl the pan around to evenly coat the inside.

3 Add the bread to the bowl and gently press to soak up the egg mixture (kind of like a sponge!), turning a few times.

4 One piece at a time, lift the soaked bread out of the egg mixture and allow the excess to drip off, then carefully place in the pan. Cook for 2 to 3 minutes on each side, or until golden and cooked through, then transfer to plates and spread with the nut butter.

5 Roughly mash half the raspberries with the yogurt, then divide between plates, scattering on the rest of the berries.

6 Pick, chop and sprinkle on the mint leaves (if using) and drizzle lightly with honey to finish.

Bonus flavor

Adding a good pinch of ground cinnamon to the egg mixture before you cook it will take the flavor to the next level. Give it a try!

FAMILY FAVORITES

Serves 4 Minutes 45

Quick and easy pizzas

With your favorite topping combo

You need

2 cloves of garlic

olive oil

1 x 14.5-oz can of whole tomatoes

3 cups self-rising flour (see note on page 118), plus extra for dusting

3 oz mozzarella cheese

optional: 4 small pork sausages

4 handfuls of your favorite vegetables, such as bell peppers, cherry tomatoes, corn kernels, broccoli, onion, and black olives

1 Peel and thinly slice the garlic, then place in a saucepan over medium heat with 1 tablespoon of olive oil and fry until golden.

2 Use your hands to crush in the tomatoes (or pour in and break up with a spoon as you go), simmer for 5 minutes, or until thickened slightly, then season to taste with sea salt and black pepper. Remove from the heat.

3 Preheat the oven to 425°F and coat two baking sheets with olive oil.

4 Add the flour to a mixing bowl, add a pinch of salt, then make a well in the middle. Pour in 1 cup of water, then use a fork to stir and bring in the flour from the outside to form a dough – when the dough starts to come together, dust your hands with flour and pat it into a ball.

5 Knead on a lightly-floured surface for a few minutes, or until smooth and elastic. Divide the dough into 4, then roll and stretch the pieces into 8-inch rounds or ovals.

6 Spread each dough round generously with the tomato sauce and tear on the mozzarella. Squeeze the sausage meat (if using) out of the casings and tear over the pizzas, then prep and scatter on your chosen vegetable toppings.

7 Transfer your pizzas to the baking sheets, drizzle lightly with olive oil, then cook in the oven for 10 minutes, or until golden and puffed up. Delicious served with a crunchy green salad.

Time-saver alert!

If you have any all-purpose tomato sauce (see page 132) left over, feel free to swap it in here to save yourself time.

"You can swap in veg oil for olive oil, if that's what you've got, and Cheddar or red Leicester for mozzarella."

Serves **4** Minutes **30**

Chicken fajitas

With zingy corn salsa

You need

1 large red onion

1 large red bell pepper

2 x 5-oz boneless, skinless chicken breasts

1 teaspoon sweet smoked paprika

½ teaspoon ground cumin

olive oil

1 ear of corn, husked

2 scallions

½ a red chili, sliced into rounds

½ a bunch of cilantro (about ½ oz)

1 lime

8 small whole wheat flour tortillas

1 little gem or ¼ of a head of iceberg lettuce

2 oz Cheddar cheese

⅓ cup plain yogurt

1. Peel and thinly slice the onion, seed and thinly slice the pepper and thinly slice the chicken, then transfer it all to a large mixing bowl.
2. Add the paprika, cumin, 1 teaspoon of olive oil and a pinch each of sea salt and black pepper, then toss together.
3. To make the corn salsa, char the corn in a dry non-stick frying pan over high heat for 8 minutes, turning regularly. Let cool, then carefully slice the kernels off the cob.
4. Place the corn kernels in a bowl, then finely chop and add the scallions, chili and 1 sprig of cilantro. Squeeze in half the lime juice, mix well and season with a little pepper. Slice the leftover lime half into wedges for serving.
5. Warm the tortillas in the microwave (keep warm until needed), shred the lettuce, grate the cheese and pick the remaining cilantro leaves.
6. Place the large non-stick frying pan over high heat, then add the chicken and vegetables and cook for 5 minutes, or until the chicken is golden and cooked through, stirring regularly.
7. Carefully take the pan of sizzling chicken and vegetables to the table (place a trivet underneath!) with the tortillas, corn salsa, lettuce, grated cheese, cilantro leaves, yogurt and lime wedges and get everyone to load up their own fajitas.

“This is one of my absolute favorite things to cook when my friends come over – so quick and easy!”

Serves 4 Minutes 35

The ultimate burger

With melty cheese and salad

You need

4 pickles

2 ripe tomatoes

¼ of a head of red cabbage (about 8 oz)

red wine vinegar

½ a head of iceberg lettuce

½ an English cucumber

extra virgin olive oil

1 x 15-oz can of lentils

8 oz ground beef or ground meat alternative

olive oil

4 slices of Cheddar cheese (about 2 oz total)

4 small burger buns

optional: ketchup and/or mayo

1 Slice the pickles (use a crinkle-cut knife, if you've got one) and tomatoes and set aside. Thinly slice or grate the cabbage, then toss in a mixing bowl with 1 tablespoon of red wine vinegar.

2 Shred the lettuce and slice the cucumber, then place in another mixing bowl and dress with 1 tablespoon of extra virgin olive oil.

3 Drain the lentils and pat dry with paper towels, then blitz in a food processor with the ground meat and a pinch of black pepper. Divide the mixture into 4 equal portions and shape into generous 1-inch-thick patties.

4 Place a large non-stick frying pan over medium heat. Brush the patties with 1 tablespoon of olive oil, then carefully place in the hot pan and cook for 4 minutes on each side, or until just cooked through, nudging the patties towards the edge of the pan to sear the sides.

5 When the patties are nearly done, place a slice of cheese on top of each one, add a splash of water to the pan (the steam will help the cheese melt), then cover and cook for another minute, or until melted.

6 Cut the buns in half (toast them if you like), add a dollop of ketchup and/or mayo (if using) to each bun bottom, then place a patty on top.

7 Layer the pickle, tomato and cucumber slices and a pinch of lettuce on top of each one, then pop the tops on. Serve the rest of the lettuce, cucumber and tomato on the side along with the pickled cabbage.

"Homemade burgers are fast, fun and juicier than the ones you buy. Plus, you can stack up the toppings and layer in your favorite sauces exactly as you like them."

Serves 4 Minutes 35

Tasty tomato soup

With melty cheese dunkers

You need

1 carrot

1 onion

1 clove of garlic

1 stalk of celery

olive oil

2 cups hot vegetable or chicken broth

1 x 28-oz can of whole tomatoes

4 slices of bread

3 oz Cheddar cheese

a few sprigs of basil

¾ cup milk

1 tablespoon balsamic vinegar

1. Peel and chop the carrot, onion and garlic, then trim and thinly slice the celery. Place a large saucepan over medium heat, drizzle in 1 tablespoon of olive oil, then scrape in the chopped vegetables.
2. Cook for 10 minutes with the lid on (leaving a little gap), or until softened, stirring occasionally, then carefully add the broth.
3. Use your hands to crush in the tomatoes (or pour in and break up with a spoon as you go), then turn up the heat to high and bring to a boil. Turn down the heat to low, pop the lid back on and simmer for 10 minutes, or until thickened slightly, stirring occasionally.
4. Toast one side of the bread slices on a baking sheet or broiler pan under the broiler until golden, flip over, then coarsely grate on the Cheddar and place back under the broiler until oozy and melty.
5. Remove the pan from the heat, pick in most of the basil leaves and pour in the milk and balsamic, then carefully blitz with an immersion blender until smooth (use a kitchen towel to protect your hands from little splashes).
6. Taste and season with sea salt and black pepper, if needed, then ladle the soup into serving bowls or mugs. Slice the toast into soldiers and serve on the side for dunking.

Time-saver alert!

Although prepping vegetables is a great way to practice your knife skills, if you want to save time, swap the whole carrot, onion and celery for 1½ cups of pre-chopped fresh or frozen mixed onion, carrot and celery – you can find this in many grocery stores.

Serves 6 | Hours 2 | Minutes 15

Barbecue ribs

With a sticky-sweet glaze

You need

optional: 1 fresh red chili

generous 1-inch piece of ginger

2 cloves of garlic

⅔ cup unsweetened apple juice

scant ½ cup white wine vinegar

2 tablespoons ketchup

1 tablespoon Dijon mustard

2 tablespoons reduced-sodium soy sauce

5 tablespoons runny honey

olive oil

2 racks of baby-back ribs (about 3½ lbs)

1 Preheat the oven to 400°F. Seed and finely chop the chili (if using), peel and grate the ginger and garlic, then place it all in a medium saucepan. Add the apple juice, vinegar, ketchup, mustard, soy and honey, and whisk together. Cook the marinade over medium heat for 10 minutes, or until thickened slightly.

2 Drizzle a little olive oil over the ribs, season with black pepper and rub all over to coat, then place in a large roasting pan lined with a double layer of aluminum foil.

3 Brush the marinade all over the ribs, then cover the pan tightly with foil. Roast for 30 minutes, then remove the pan from the oven, take off the foil, and baste. Preheat your grill to medium-low at this stage (if using; see step 5).

4 Carefully put the foil back on and return the ribs to the oven for another 30 minutes, or until the meat pulls easily away from the bone.

5 Remove the pan from the oven and discard the foil, baste again, then either return to the oven, uncovered, for 15 minutes, or transfer to the grill and cook over medium-low heat for 5 to 10 minutes, or until beautifully sticky and caramelized.

6 Transfer the ribs to a board, slice up and serve. Delicious with a crunchy green salad and new potatoes.

Serves 2-4 Minutes 30

Easy fish cakes

With Cheddar, lemon and parsley

You need

1 ¼ lbs potatoes

olive oil

1 x 8-oz skinless salmon fillets, pin-boned

a few sprigs of Italian parsley

1 lemon

2 oz Cheddar cheese

3 tablespoons all-purpose flour

1 Peel the potatoes, chop into generous 1-inch chunks and cook in a pot of boiling salted water for 12 minutes, or until tender.

2 Drizzle 1 tablespoon of olive oil into a large non-stick frying pan over medium heat, add the salmon and cook for 6 to 8 minutes, or until just cooked through, turning regularly, then let cool.

3 Pick and finely chop the parsley, finely grate the lemon zest and coarsely grate the Cheddar.

4 Drain the potatoes and let steam dry for a few minutes, then return to the pot and mash with a potato masher.

5 Scrape in the parsley, lemon zest and Cheddar, season with a pinch each of sea salt and black pepper, then mix together. Flake in the salmon and fold in, shape into 4 patties, then coat all over with the flour.

6 Place the pan back over medium heat and cook the fish cakes for 3 minutes on each side, or until beautifully golden.

7 Cut the lemon into wedges for squeezing. Delicious served with a green salad or peas.

Flavor switch-up

You can take this basic recipe in lots of different directions by simply adding or swapping in one or two ingredients. Why not try adding a little curry paste or some fresh chili for a bit of a kick, or switch up the herbs (basil, mint, cilantro or chives are delicious). You can use tinned fish in place of the fresh salmon, if you prefer, and a handful of cooked chopped shrimp thrown into the mix are really yummy, too.

Serves 2 Hours 1

Crispy chicken

With slaw, corn and potato wedges

You need

1–2 thick slices of whole wheat bread (about 3 oz)

½ a clove of garlic

2 x 5-oz boneless, skinless chicken breasts

1 lb Yukon Gold potatoes

olive oil

2 ears of corn, husked

½ a red onion

1 small carrot

½ an apple

¼ of a head of green cabbage (about 8 oz)

½ teaspoon Dijon or English mustard

½ tablespoon extra virgin olive oil

1 tablespoon white wine vinegar

2 generous tablespoons plain yogurt

1. Preheat the oven to 400°F. Tear the bread into a food processor, peel and add the garlic, then whiz until fine.
2. Place the chicken breasts between two sheets of parchment paper, then use a rolling pin or the base of a heavy pan to pound and flatten them out to about ½ inch thick.
3. Lift up the pounded chicken breasts, pour half the breadcrumbs onto the paper, put the chicken back on top, and sprinkle with the rest of the crumbs. Roughly pat the breadcrumbs onto the chicken, then re-cover with the paper and pound again to help them stick.
4. Scrub the potatoes, then slice into wedges (use a crinkle-cut knife, if you've got one) and add to a large mixing bowl. Season with a pinch each of sea salt and black pepper and drizzle with 1 tablespoon of olive oil, then toss to coat.
5. Spread out in a single layer on a large baking sheet and bake for 35 minutes, or until golden and cooked through, giving the pan a shake and adding the corn to the oven for the last 10 minutes.
6. Peel the onion and coarsely grate on a box grater or in a food processor (or slice by hand) with the carrot, apple (discarding the core) and cabbage. Add to a mixing bowl, stir in the mustard, extra virgin olive oil, vinegar and yogurt, then season to taste.
7. When the potatoes have 10 minutes to go, place a large non-stick frying pan over medium heat with 1 tablespoon of olive oil and fry the chicken for 3 minutes on each side, or until golden and cooked through, adding an extra drizzle of oil, if needed.
8. Transfer the chicken to a board, slice ½ inch thick, and serve with the potato wedges, corn and slaw. Delicious with ketchup for dipping.

Serves 6 | Hours 1 | Minutes 20

Buddy's Bolognese

With sausages, ground beef and grated vegetables

You need

2 pork sausages

olive oil

1 lb lean ground beef

2 onions

2 cloves of garlic

1 large carrot

1 stalk of celery

1 zucchini

2 tablespoons balsamic glaze

1 x 28-oz can of whole tomatoes

1 heaping teaspoon tomato paste

1 lb of your favorite dried pasta

Parmesan cheese, to serve

1. Place a large Dutch oven over medium-high heat to warm up.
2. Squeeze the sausage meat out of the casings.
3. Drizzle 1 tablespoon of olive oil into the pot, add the ground beef and sausage meat, breaking everything up with a spoon as you go, then cook for 5 minutes, stirring regularly.
4. Peel the onions and garlic, trim the carrot, celery and zucchini, then coarsely grate all the vegetables on a box grater, finely grating the garlic. Scrape into the pot, then turn down the heat to medium-low and cook for 10 minutes, or until softened, stirring occasionally.
5. Add the balsamic glaze, then use your hands to crush in the tomatoes (or pour in and break up with a spoon as you go). Fill the can halfway with water, swirl around to pick up the last bits of tomato and pour it into the pot.
6. Stir in the tomato paste and a pinch of black pepper, mash everything up with the spoon, then turn down the heat to low and cook for 1 hour, or until thickened slightly.
7. About 15 minutes before you're ready to serve, cook the pasta in a large pot of boiling salted water following the package instructions, then drain, reserving a generous cupful of starchy cooking water.
8. Carefully add the pasta to the sauce and stir well over the heat, loosening with a splash of pasta water, if needed. Divide between serving bowls and finish with a good grating of Parmesan.

Serves 8 Hours 1

Green crêpe stack

Creamy spinach sauce, cheese and ham

You need

2 large eggs

1 ¼ cups all-purpose flour

3 ½ cups milk

6 cups baby spinach (about 6 oz)

4 tablespoons unsalted butter (½ a stick)

2 cloves of garlic

olive oil

6 oz Cheddar cheese

optional: 4 oz smoked ham

1 head of butter or bibb lettuce

red wine vinegar

Easy swaps

Dress the salad with whatever vinegar and oil you have in the cupboard.

1 Preheat the oven to 350°F. For the crêpes, crack the eggs into a blender, add 1 cup of flour, ⅔ cup of milk, 1 cup of spinach and a pinch each of sea salt and black pepper, then blitz until smooth.

2 Melt the butter in a saucepan over medium heat, then peel, thinly slice and add the garlic and cook for 2 minutes, or until softened.

3 Stir in the remaining flour and gradually pour in the remaining milk, then cook until thickened slightly. Stir in the remaining spinach and season to taste.

4 Put a 10-inch non-stick frying pan over medium heat with 1 tablespoon of olive oil. Add just enough batter to coat the base of the pan, gently swirling it to cover, cook until lightly golden, then flip and cook on the other side. Repeat with the remaining batter, wiping out the pan with a ball of paper towels and adding a tiny drizzle of oil each time – you should end up with 5 thin crêpes.

5 Meanwhile, grate the cheese and tear up the ham (if using).

6 If your frying pan isn't ovenproof, get yourself a deep ovenproof pan or dish (10 inches in diameter). Add and repeat layers of crêpe, spinach sauce, ham and cheese until you've used up all the ingredients, finishing with a layer of sauce and cheese.

7 Bake for 30 minutes, or until golden and bubbling, then let rest for 10 minutes before serving.

8 Separate out the lettuce leaves, toss with 3 tablespoons of olive oil and 1 tablespoon of red wine vinegar, then season to taste and serve alongside the crêpe stack.

Serves 4-6 | Hours 1

Sausage and bean casserole

With peppers and gentle spices

You need

6 pork or veggie sausages

2 red onions

2 cloves of garlic

2 stalks of celery

2 red bell peppers

olive oil

2 teaspoons sweet smoked paprika

1 teaspoon ground cumin

1 tablespoon steak sauce

1 x 28-oz can of whole tomatoes

2 x 15-oz cans of cannellini beans

optional: a few sprigs of Italian parsley

1 Preheat the broiler to medium. Prick the sausages, then broil on a baking sheet or broiler pan for 10 minutes, or until browned all over, turning halfway. Transfer to paper towels to drain, patting them dry.

2 Peel the onions and garlic, trim the celery and seed the peppers, then roughly chop. Drizzle 1 tablespoon of olive oil into a large Dutch oven over medium heat, add the chopped vegetables, then cook for 10 minutes, or until softened, stirring regularly.

3 Add the paprika, cumin and steak sauce and cook for another 2 minutes. Use your hands to crush in the tomatoes (or pour in and break up with a spoon as you go). Fill the can halfway with water, swirl it around to pick up the last bits of tomato and pour it into the pot.

4 Add the beans (juices and all), stir well, then bring to a boil while you slice up the sausages and add them to the pot.

5 Turn down the heat to low and cook for 40 minutes, or until thickened slightly, adding splashes of water to loosen, if needed. Taste and season with sea salt and black pepper, if needed, then pick and tear in the parsley (if using). Tasty served with green veggies and perfect rice (see page 138), mashed potatoes or baked potatoes (see page 142).

“If I've got any stale bread hanging around, I sometimes whiz it into fine breadcrumbs, toast until golden and sprinkle over the top before tucking in.”

Serves 4 Minutes 45

Fish stick sandwiches

With sweet potato fries

You need

4 sweet potatoes (about 1¾ lbs total)

1 teaspoon sweet smoked paprika

olive oil

¼ cup all-purpose flour

1 large egg

1–2 thick slices of whole wheat bread (about 3 oz)

optional: ½ oz Cheddar or Parmesan cheese

4 x 4-oz skinless white fish or salmon fillets, pin-boned

2 tablespoons ketchup

generous ¼ cup plain yogurt

1 little gem lettuce

4 sub rolls

1 Preheat the oven to 400°F. Scrub the sweet potatoes, slice each one into chunky wedges (use a crinkle-cut knife, if you've got one), then transfer them to a large baking sheet.

2 Season lightly with sea salt, black pepper and the paprika, then drizzle with 1 tablespoon of olive oil and toss to coat. Spread out in a single layer on the sheet and bake for 35 minutes, or until golden and cooked through.

3 Sprinkle the flour onto a plate and beat the egg in a shallow bowl. Whiz the bread in a food processor with the cheese (if using), 2 tablespoons of olive oil and a pinch each of salt and pepper until fine, then transfer to a plate or baking sheet. Line a second sheet with parchment paper.

4 Carefully slice each fish fillet in half lengthwise (it doesn't matter if they're slightly different shapes). Dip each one in the flour, turning to coat evenly, dip into the egg, letting any excess drip off, then roll in the breadcrumbs until well coated all over.

5 Transfer to the prepared pan (or at this stage you can freeze the fish sticks, so feel free to double the recipe and have some extras for another day).

6 When the potatoes have 15 minutes to go, add the pan of fish sticks to the oven and bake until golden and cooked through (bake them for 20 minutes if cooking straight from frozen).

7 Mix the ketchup and yogurt together to make a sauce, trim and finely shred the lettuce, and slice the rolls in half.

8 Load up the bottoms of the rolls with a spoonful of the sauce and a handful of shredded lettuce, then place 2 fish sticks on each one and pop the tops on. Serve the sweet potato fries alongside.

Serves 6 Hours 1

Vegetable curry

With cooling cucumber yogurt

You need

1 ¼ lbs butternut squash

2 tablespoons curry powder

½ a bunch of cilantro (about ½ oz)

2 onions

2 cloves of garlic

generous 1-inch piece of ginger

¼ of a head of cauliflower (about 8 oz)

4 ripe tomatoes

olive oil

⅔ cup hot vegetable broth

1 x 14-oz can of lite coconut milk

1 x 15-oz can of chickpeas

½ an English cucumber

½ a bunch of mint (about ½ oz)

⅔ cup plain yogurt

1 lemon

3 cups baby spinach (about 3 oz)

1 Peel and seed the squash, chop into ¾-inch chunks, then toss in a mixing bowl with 1 tablespoon of curry powder and a pinch each of sea salt and black pepper.

2 Pick the cilantro leaves and finely chop the stems. Peel and thinly slice the onions, then peel and finely chop the garlic and ginger. Slice the cauliflower into florets, thinly slicing any stems, and roughly chop the tomatoes.

3 Drizzle 1 tablespoon of olive oil into a large saucepan over medium heat, add the squash and cook for 6 minutes, or until softened, stirring occasionally, then transfer to a plate.

4 Place the pan back over medium heat with 1 tablespoon of olive oil, the cilantro stems, the remaining 1 tablespoon of curry powder, and the onion, garlic and ginger. Cook for 5 minutes, stirring occasionally.

5 Carefully pour in the broth along with the coconut milk. Add the tomatoes, squash and chickpeas (juices and all), then cook over low heat for 30 minutes, or until thickened slightly, adding the cauliflower for the last 10 minutes.

6 To make the cucumber yogurt, halve the cucumber lengthwise and scrape out the seeds, then coarsely grate into a bowl. Pick, finely chop and add the mint leaves, then stir in the yogurt and a squeeze of lemon juice. Taste and season, if needed.

7 When the time's up on the curry, stir in the spinach and let wilt, then taste and adjust the seasoning, if needed.

8 Sprinkle with the cilantro leaves and serve with the cucumber yogurt, perfect rice (see page 138) and the remaining lemon sliced into wedges for squeezing.

EAT THE
SEASONS

Serves 4 Minutes 35

Spring vegetable noodle stir-fry

With toasted peanut sprinkle

You need

1 red onion

4 cloves of garlic

2½-inch piece of ginger

½ a bunch of cilantro (about ½ oz)

1 red bell pepper

1 carrot

6 oz asparagus

4 oz baby zucchini (or 1 small zucchini)

8 oz medium stir-fry egg noodles

optional: ½ a red chili

1 lime

¾ cup unsalted peanuts

olive oil

4 oz sugar snap peas or snow peas

¼ cup reduced-sodium low-salt soy sauce

1 Peel the onion and garlic and thinly slice, then peel and matchstick the ginger. Pick the cilantro leaves and finely chop the stems.

2 Seed and thinly slice the pepper, and scrub and thinly slice the carrot. Snap the woody ends off the asparagus and slice into generous 1-inch pieces along with the baby zucchini (or slice if using a regular zucchini).

3 Cook the noodles following the package instructions, then drain and refresh in cold water (this prevents them from overcooking).

4 Trim, seed and finely chop the chili (if using), and halve the lime.

5 Place a large non-stick frying pan (or wok) over medium heat, add the peanuts and toast until golden, then transfer to a board.

6 With the pan still over high heat, drizzle in 1 tablespoon of olive oil, then add the onion, garlic, ginger, chili and cilantro stems and stir-fry for 2 minutes, or until lightly golden.

7 Add the pepper, carrot, asparagus and zucchini, fry for another 3 minutes, then add the sugar snaps or snow peas and the noodles for 1 final minute. Squeeze in half the lime juice and add the soy, then toss everything together.

8 Divide between plates, sprinkle with the cilantro leaves, then chop and sprinkle on the toasted nuts. Cut the remaining lime into wedges for squeezing.

“I’ve used spring vegetables here, but feel free to swap in different veggies depending on the time of year, or what you have to use up.”

Serves 12 Hours 1

Plus proofing

New potato and pesto focaccia

With oozy mozzarella

You need

2 ¼ teaspoons instant or rapid-rise yeast

3 ½ cups bread flour, plus extra for dusting

olive oil, for greasing

8 oz baby new potatoes

6 tablespoons fine dried breadcrumbs

1 x 4-oz ball of mozzarella cheese

½ cup of your favorite pesto (see page 130)

1 Stir the yeast into 1 ¼ cups of lukewarm water and let sit for a few minutes. Add the flour to a large mixing bowl, stir in 1 teaspoon of sea salt, then make a well in the middle. Pour in the yeast mixture, then use a fork to bring in the flour from the outside to form a dough.

2 Knead on a lightly-floured surface for 10 minutes, or until smooth and springy. Place in a lightly-oiled bowl, then cover with a clean, damp kitchen towel and let rise in a warm place for 1 hour, or until doubled in size.

3 Scrub the potatoes, halving any larger ones, then cook in a saucepan of boiling salted water over medium heat for 12 minutes, or until tender. Drain and let cool in a colander.

4 Lightly grease a 9 x 13-inch roasting pan, then sprinkle in the bread-crumbs and shake around so they stick to the oil.

5 Knead and punch the dough, knocking all the air out of it, then stretch it out to fill the pan. Use your fingers to gently push down and create lots of dips and wells.

6 Transfer the potatoes to a mixing bowl and tear in the mozzarella, then add the pesto and toss together, breaking up some of the potatoes as you go. Spread this topping mixture evenly over the dough, drizzle with 2 tablespoons of olive oil, then press the topping down into the dips and wells, seasoning from a height with salt and black pepper.

7 Cover the dish with a clean, damp kitchen towel, then let rise in a warm place for 1 hour, or until doubled in size.

8 Preheat the oven to 425°F. Very carefully – to keep the air in the dough – place the pan directly on the bottom of the oven and bake for 25 to 30 minutes, or until golden and cooked through.

Serves 4 Minutes 45

Summery salmon bake

New potatoes, tomatoes, beans, peas and pesto

You need

8 oz green beans

1 lb baby new potatoes

1 ¼ cups cherry tomatoes

1 ½ cups frozen peas

olive oil

4 x 4-oz skin-on salmon fillets, scaled, pin-boned

½ a bunch of basil (about ½ oz)

¼ cup of your favorite pesto (see page 130)

1 lemon

1. Preheat the oven to 400°F. Trim the green beans and scrub the potatoes, halving any larger ones.
2. Cook the potatoes in a saucepan of boiling salted water over high heat for 12 minutes, adding the green beans for the last 2 minutes, then drain and transfer to a 9 x 13-inch baking dish.
3. Halve the tomatoes and scatter into the dish along with the frozen peas. Drizzle with 1 tablespoon of olive oil and season with a pinch each of sea salt and black pepper, then toss together, and shake into a nice even layer.
4. Arrange the salmon fillets on top, skin-side up, and roast for 15 minutes, or until the salmon is just cooked through and the skin is crispy.
5. Divide between plates, drizzling on any juices from the baking dish, then pick and sprinkle on the basil leaves. Finish with dollops of pesto, and cut the lemon into wedges for squeezing.

“This is one of my favorite ways to enjoy salmon – throw it together and get it in the oven.”

Serves 2 Minutes 20

Grilled chicken lollipops

With pepper and pineapple salsa and lemony couscous

You need

¾ cup whole wheat couscous

olive oil

2 lemons

2 x 5-oz boneless, skinless chicken breasts

4 sprigs of rosemary (tied together with a piece of string)

1 teaspoon runny honey

1 red bell pepper

¼ of a small red onion

1 scant cup chopped fresh pineapple

optional: ½ a bunch of soft herbs, such as mint or Italian parsley (about ½ oz)

¼ cup plain yogurt

1 Soak 6 wooden skewers in cold water to prevent them from burning later on.

2 Place the couscous in a bowl with ½ tablespoon of olive oil. Finely grate in the zest of ½ a lemon and squeeze in the juice, throwing the squeezed half into the bowl. Just cover the couscous with boiling water, then cover and set aside to fluff up.

3 Carefully push 3 skewers horizontally into each chicken breast (trim the skewers, if needed), season with black pepper, squeeze on the juice of ½ a lemon and drizzle with ½ tablespoon of olive oil.

4 You can cook the skewers on a hot grill or in a non-stick frying pan on the stove. Either way, cook them for 8 to 10 minutes, or until the chicken is golden and cooked through, turning regularly. For the final minute of cooking, use the rosemary sprigs to brush the honey over the chicken, giving it a lovely sticky glaze.

5 Halve, seed and finely chop the pepper, then peel and finely chop the onion and finely chop the pineapple and scrape everything into a bowl. Add a squeeze of lemon juice and a drizzle of olive oil, then taste and season with sea salt and pepper, if needed. Pick and finely chop the herbs (if using), then add to the bowl and toss together.

6 Fluff up the couscous with a fork, season to taste with salt and pepper, and divide between plates.

7 Slice the chicken between the skewers, making sure it's cooked through – if it's not, cook it a little longer. Place 3 chicken lollipops on each plate and portion out the salsa. Serve with yogurt for dipping, and cut the remaining lemon into wedges for squeezing.

Serves **4-6** Minutes **55**

Autumn veggie chili

Sweet potatoes, peppers and eggplant

You need

1 lb sweet potatoes

2 mixed-color bell peppers

1 eggplant

1 onion

2 cloves of garlic

1 bunch of cilantro (about 1 oz)

olive oil

1 teaspoon chili powder

1 teaspoon ground cinnamon

2 teaspoons ground cumin

1 x 15-oz can of kidney beans

1 x 15-oz can of chickpeas

1 x 28-oz can of whole tomatoes

4–6 tablespoons plain yogurt

1. Peel the sweet potatoes and seed the peppers, then chop into bite-size chunks along with the eggplant.
2. Peel and roughly chop the onion and peel and finely chop the garlic, then pick the cilantro leaves, finely chopping the stems.
3. Drizzle 1 tablespoon of olive oil into a large Dutch oven over medium heat, then add all the chopped ingredients and cook for 15 minutes with the lid on (leaving a little gap), stirring occasionally.
4. Stir in the spices and cook for 2 minutes, then drain and add the beans and chickpeas. Use your hands to crush in the tomatoes (or pour in and break up with a spoon as you go).
5. Bring to a boil, then cook for 30 minutes over low heat, or until thickened slightly, adding splashes of water to loosen, if needed.
6. Stir in most of the cilantro leaves, then taste and season with sea salt and black pepper, if needed. Sprinkle the rest of the cilantro leaves over the top and serve with the yogurt for dolloping.

“I love this with perfect rice (see page 138) or served up on a baked potato (see page 142), or you can spoon it into a wrap or dollop it over nachos (see page 124). Yum!”

Serves 2 Minutes 25

Smashed squash quesadilla

With avocado yogurt and lime

You need

1 lb fresh or frozen butternut squash

1 teaspoon sweet smoked paprika

6 scallions

1 oz Cheddar cheese

2 whole wheat or seeded tortillas

½ a ripe avocado

2 generous tablespoons plain yogurt

½ a lime

1. If using fresh, peel the squash and chop into ¾-inch chunks (seed first, if needed), then transfer to a microwave-safe dish and cook in the microwave on high for 7 minutes, or until tender. If using frozen, defrost the squash in the microwave for 5 minutes, then cook on high for another 5 minutes, or until tender.
2. Mash the cooked squash with the paprika and a pinch each of sea salt and black pepper.
3. Place a large non-stick frying pan over medium heat to warm up while you trim and thinly slice the scallions and grate the Cheddar.
4. Sprinkle half the cheese and scallions over one tortilla and top with the mashed squash. Sprinkle on the remaining scallions and cheese, and top with the second tortilla, pressing down slightly.
5. Carefully transfer to the hot pan and cook for 3 minutes, then flip and continue cooking for 1 to 2 minutes, or until golden and crisp. Slide onto a board and cut into 8 wedges.
6. Mash the avocado (pit if needed) with the yogurt and serve on the side for dunking. Slice the lime into wedges for squeezing.

Serves 4-6 | Hours 1 | Minutes 20

Winter chicken hot pot

With a cheat's sauce and sausages

You need

2 onions

2 carrots

4 boneless, skinless chicken thighs

4 small pork sausages

olive oil

2 x 10.5-oz cans of cream of chicken and mushroom soup

1 ¼ lbs potatoes

1 teaspoon dried thyme

1 Peel and roughly chop the onions and carrots, and chop the chicken and sausages into generous 1-inch chunks.

2 Drizzle 1 tablespoon of olive oil into a small (10-inch) Dutch oven, add the chopped vegetables, chicken and sausages and cook for 15 minutes, or until lightly golden.

3 Pour in the soup and mix well, then simmer over low heat for 10 minutes, or until thickened slightly.

4 Preheat the oven to 350°F. Scrub and slice the potatoes so they're just under ¼ inch thick (or feed them through the thick slicer attachment of a food processor to speed things up).

5 Toss the sliced potatoes with a pinch each of sea salt and black pepper, 1 tablespoon of olive oil and the thyme. Carefully layer the potatoes over the stew so it's completely covered, overlapping them slightly.

6 Bake for 40 minutes, or until the potatoes are golden and tender. Delicious served with green beans, broccoli or peas.

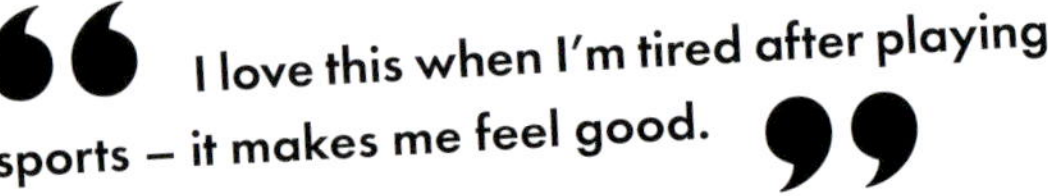

Serves 2 Minutes 25

Steak sandwich

With crunchy winter slaw

You need

1 x 8-oz sirloin steak, trimmed

olive oil

1 sprig of rosemary

2 small ciabatta rolls

unsalted butter, for spreading

jarred horseradish, mustard, ketchup or steak sauce, to serve

Winter slaw

1 carrot

1 small parsnip

½ a small red onion

⅙ of a head of green cabbage (about 6 oz)

1 small apple

½ a lemon

⅓ cup plain yogurt

1 tablespoon grainy mustard

1 Season the steak with a pinch each of sea salt and black pepper and drizzle with 1 tablespoon of olive oil, then rub all over. Strip off and finely chop the rosemary leaves, then pat them onto the steak.

2 For the slaw, scrub and coarsely grate the carrot and parsnip, and peel and very thinly slice the onion, then scrape into a mixing bowl.

3 Remove any shriveled outer leaves from the cabbage, then very thinly slice into strips and add to the bowl.

4 Coarsely grate the apple, discarding the stem and seeds, then add to the bowl. Finely grate in the lemon zest and squeeze in the juice, then add the yogurt and mustard and mix well.

5 Place a non-stick frying pan over high heat. Once hot, carefully place the steak in the pan and cook for 2 minutes on each side for medium-rare, or until cooked to your liking, then transfer to a board to rest.

6 Halve the ciabatta rolls – you can leave them as is or toast them alongside the steak in the pan. Lightly butter the ciabatta, then spread with the condiments of your choice.

7 Drizzle the steak lightly with olive oil and slice into strips, then toss with the juices on the board and divide between the bottoms of the rolls.

8 Swipe the tops of the rolls through any remaining steak juices, sandwich together and cut in half. Serve with the slaw on the side, or stuff some into the sandwich, if you prefer.

I ♥
PASTA

Serves 1 · Minutes 30

Plus resting

Spicy tomato pasta

With homemade tagliatelle

You need

1 clove of garlic

olive oil

½ a red chili

2 large ripe tomatoes

1 x pasta dough (see below), 5 oz fresh pasta or 3 oz dried pasta

Pasta dough (optional)

¾ cup all-purpose flour or Tipo 00 flour, plus extra for dusting

1 large egg

1 Peel and thinly slice the garlic, then add to a saucepan over medium heat with 1 tablespoon of olive oil and cook for 1 minute, or until starting to turn golden.

2 Seed and finely chop the chili, roughly chop the tomatoes, and add both to the pan with a splash of water. Cook for 10 minutes, or until the tomatoes have broken down into a chunky sauce, stirring regularly. Season to taste with sea salt and black pepper.

3 Cook the pasta in a pot of boiling salted water for 2 to 3 minutes if making your own pasta dough, or following the package instructions, then drain, reserving a generous cupful of starchy cooking water. Carefully toss the pasta with the sauce, loosening with a splash of pasta water, if needed. Delicious served with a fine grating of Parmesan.

To make fresh pasta dough

1 For the pasta dough, add the flour to a mixing bowl and make a well in the middle. Crack in the egg, then use a fork to beat the egg until smooth. Gradually bring in the flour from the outside, adding a splash of water, if needed. When the dough starts to come together, dust your hands with flour and pat it into a ball.

2 Knead on a lightly-floured surface for 4 to 5 minutes, or until smooth and elastic (tweak with a splash more water or flour if you need to). Cover and let relax for 30 minutes.

3 Dust a clean work surface with flour, then use a rolling pin to roll out the pasta as thin as you can (aim for about 1⁄16 inch), dusting it well with flour as you go.

4 Loosely roll up the pasta sheet, then use a sharp knife to slice it just over ¼ inch wide, tossing it with your fingertips to separate the strands.

Serves 6 Hours 2

Scruffy lasagna bake

Made with Buddy's Bolognese

You need

1 x Buddy's Bolognese (see page 48)

8 oz frozen chopped spinach

8 oz fresh (or dried and cooked) lasagna sheets

⅔ cup cottage cheese

4 oz Cheddar cheese

1 Preheat the oven to 400°F. Make the Bolognese or, if already made, reheat it in a large shallow Dutch oven, with a good splash of water to loosen, then remove from the heat.

2 Add the frozen spinach to the Bolognese, then tear in the pasta sheets and mix up really well to coat and separate, pulling some of the pasta sheets to the surface to create a top layer (hiding the spinach underneath).

3 Spoon on dollops of cottage cheese, then grate on the Cheddar.

4 Bake for 25 minutes, or until golden and bubbling. Delicious served with a green salad.

> "Making a delicious lasagna feels quite grown-up, but this one is really easy."

Serves 4 Minutes 20

Greens pasta

With crispy garlicky breadcrumbs

You need

1 x 3-inch piece of fresh garlic bread

1 head of broccoli

1 bunch of scallions

3 cloves of garlic

olive oil

scant 1 cup frozen peas

4 oz frozen spinach

12 oz dried farfalle

2 oz Parmesan or Cheddar cheese, plus extra to serve

1. Pulse the garlic bread in a food processor until you have fine crumbs, then toast in a large shallow Dutch oven over medium heat until lightly golden and crisp and transfer to a small bowl.
2. Break the broccoli into bite-size florets, thinly slicing the stem. Trim and slice the scallions, and peel and finely chop the garlic.
3. Drizzle 1 tablespoon of olive oil into the pot and place back over medium heat. Add the broccoli stems, scallions and garlic, followed 2 minutes later by half the peas and all the spinach.
4. Season with a pinch each of sea salt and black pepper, then cook for 10 minutes, or until soft and the spinach has thawed, stirring regularly.
5. Meanwhile, cook the pasta in a large pot of boiling salted water following the package instructions, and adding the broccoli florets and remaining peas for the last 3 minutes. Finely grate the cheese.
6. Scoop 1 cup of the starchy cooking water from the pasta pot and stir it into the vegetables along with the cheese, then blitz carefully with an immersion blender until smooth.
7. Drain the pasta, broccoli and peas, toss with the sauce, and serve, finishing with a fine grating of cheese. Serve the garlicky breadcrumbs alongside for sprinkling.

Serves **6** · Hours **1** · Minutes **15**

Makes 30 meatballs

Plus cooling and chilling

Easy spaghetti and meatballs

With bonus grated vegetables

You need

1 onion

4 cloves of garlic

1 zucchini

6 cremini or white button mushrooms

olive oil

8 oz lean ground beef

8 oz lean ground pork

6 tablespoons fine dried breadcrumbs, preferably whole wheat

1 oz Parmesan cheese, plus extra to serve

1 large egg

1 x 24-oz jar of tomato passata

1 lb dried spaghetti

> **“Definitely one of my favorite things to make, and everyone seems to love it!”**

1. Peel the onion and 2 cloves of garlic, then coarsely grate on a box grater with the zucchini and mushrooms. Scrape everything into a large non-stick frying pan over medium heat with 1 tablespoon of olive oil and cook for 10 minutes, or until softened, stirring regularly.

2. Transfer the cooked vegetables to a mixing bowl and let cool, then add the beef, pork and breadcrumbs. Finely grate in most of the Parmesan and crack in the egg, then season with black pepper.

3. Massage the mixture together to combine, then, with wet hands, take tablespoons of the mixture and shape into 30 little balls. Pop them onto a baking sheet as you go, then chill in the fridge for 10 minutes to firm up.

4. Place the large non-stick frying pan over medium heat with 1 tablespoon of olive oil, then add the meatballs and cook for 8 to 10 minutes, or until golden brown all over, turning regularly.

5. Peel and finely chop the remaining garlic cloves. Create a little space in the pan between the meatballs, add the garlic for 2 minutes, then pour in the passata and give the pan a gentle shake.

6. Simmer for 20 minutes, or until the meatballs are cooked through and the sauce is thickened slightly, stirring occasionally. Taste and season with sea salt and pepper, if needed.

7. With around 10 minutes to go, cook the pasta in a large pot of boiling salted water following the package instructions, then drain, reserving a generous cupful of starchy cooking water.

8. Add the pasta to the meatball pan and gently toss together, loosening with a splash of pasta water, if needed. Divide between bowls, serving the meatballs on top, and finish with a grating of Parmesan.

Serves **4** Minutes **25**

Peasto pasta

With pounded chicken

You need

2½ cups frozen peas

1 small clove of garlic

1 bunch of basil or mint (about 1 oz)

¼ cup pine nuts

2 oz Parmesan or Cheddar cheese, plus extra for grating

extra virgin olive oil

1 lemon

1 lb fresh (or dried and cooked) lasagna sheets

4 x 5-oz boneless, skinless chicken breasts

olive oil

Veggie swap-in

Replace the pounded chicken with a poached egg (see page 22) or fried egg (see page 24).

1 Place the peas in a microwave-safe bowl and microwave on high for 3 minutes, stirring halfway.

2 Peel the garlic and place in a mortar and pestle with a pinch of sea salt. Pick in most of the herb leaves and grind to a paste. Add the pine nuts, finely grate in the cheese and muddle in 2 tablespoons of extra virgin olive oil. Drain and add the peas to the herby mixture, then roughly bash it all up. Squeeze in the lemon juice and season to taste.

3 Use scissors (go for crinkle-cut scissors, if you have them) to cut the lasagna sheets into fun shapes, tearing up the scraps, then set aside.

4 Place the chicken breasts between two sheets of parchment paper, then use a rolling pin or the base of a heavy pan to pound and flatten them out to around ½ inch thick.

5 Place a large non-stick frying pan over medium heat with 1 tablespoon of olive oil, fry the chicken for 3 minutes on each side, or until golden and cooked through, then transfer to a plate to rest – you'll need to work in batches.

6 If using fresh pasta, cook the pasta in a large pot of boiling salted water for 2 to 3 minutes, or until tender, then drain, reserving a generous cupful of starchy cooking water. Carefully toss the pasta with the peasto, loosening with splashes of pasta water, if needed.

7 Plate up the pasta, slice the chicken and arrange on top, and finish with the remaining herbs and an extra grating of cheese, if you like.

Cauliflower mac and cheese

Topped with crispy breadcrumbs

You need

optional: 3 slices of smoked bacon or 6 slices of pancetta

3 cloves of garlic

olive oil

3 tablespoons all-purpose flour

5½ cups reduced-fat milk

1 tablespoon Dijon or English mustard

1 head of cauliflower (about 1¾ lbs)

1 lb dried elbow macaroni

6 oz Cheddar cheese

2 thick slices of bread

1 sprig of rosemary

1 Preheat the oven to 375°F. Lay the bacon or pancetta (if using) in a 9 x 13-inch baking dish, roast for 10 minutes, then remove.

2 Peel and finely chop the garlic, then add to a large shallow Dutch oven over medium heat with 3 tablespoons of olive oil. Stir in the flour and very gradually pour in the milk, simmer for 5 minutes, or until thickened slightly, then stir in the mustard.

3 Remove and discard any shriveled outer leaves from the cauliflower, then break the rest into bite-size pieces (including the leaves, removing any super-tough stalks).

4 Cook the pasta in a large pot of boiling salted water for 7 minutes, add the cauliflower and cook for another 5 minutes, then drain.

5 Grate most of the Cheddar into the white sauce and mix well, then stir in the cauliflower and pasta, breaking up the cauliflower slightly with a potato masher as you go.

6 Place the cooked bacon or pancetta in a food processor with 1 tablespoon of olive oil and the bread. Strip in the rosemary and blitz to coarse breadcrumbs.

7 Transfer the pasta mixture to the baking dish, grate on the remaining cheese and sprinkle with the breadcrumbs. Bake for 25 minutes, or until golden and bubbling. Delicious served with a green salad.

Serves 2 Minutes 25

Tuna pasta

With tomatoes, leeks, fresh chili and basil

You need

1 leek

optional: ½ a red chili

1 clove of garlic

olive oil

1 x 14.5-oz can of whole tomatoes

1 x 4-oz can of tuna in spring water

6 oz dried spaghetti

2 sprigs of basil

Parmesan cheese, to serve

1 Halve, wash and thinly slice the white part of the leek (save the green part for making stock or soup). Seed and finely chop the chili (if using), and peel and finely chop the garlic.

2 Place a large non-stick frying pan over medium heat with ½ tablespoon of olive oil, add the chopped vegetables and cook for 5 minutes, or until softened, stirring regularly.

3 Use your hands to crush in the tomatoes (or pour in and break up with a spoon as you go). Fill the can one-quarter full with water, swirl it around to pick up the last bits of tomato and pour it into the pan.

4 Drain and flake in the tuna, season with a pinch each of sea salt and black pepper, then bring to a boil. Turn down the heat to low and let simmer while you cook your pasta, stirring occasionally.

5 Cook the pasta in a large pot of boiling salted water following the package instructions, then drain, reserving a generous cupful of the starchy cooking water. Carefully add the pasta to the sauce and stir well over the heat, loosening with a splash of pasta water, if needed.

6 Divide between bowls, then pick and tear on the basil leaves and finish with a good grating of Parmesan.

Serves 4 Minutes 15

Portable pasta salad

Crunchy vegetables, fresh basil and feta

You need

12 oz dried penne or pasta shells

½ an English cucumber

1 red bell pepper

1 lb ripe tomatoes

optional: 1 handful of olives

½ a bunch of basil (about ½ oz)

extra virgin olive oil

red wine vinegar

4 oz feta cheese

1. Cook the pasta in a large pot of boiling salted water following the package instructions.
2. Slice the cucumber in half lengthwise, scoop out and discard the seeds, then slice in half again. Chop into small pieces and add to a mixing bowl.
3. Seed the pepper and chop to roughly the same size as the cucumber. Coarsely grate the tomatoes, discarding any tough skin and excess seeds, then add to the bowl.
4. Pit and tear in the olives (if using) along with the basil leaves, then add 1 tablespoon of extra virgin olive oil and 1 teaspoon of red wine vinegar.
5. Drain the pasta and refresh under cold running water, then add to the bowl and toss everything together well. Season to taste with sea salt and black pepper and crumble on the feta to serve.

AFTER-SCHOOL BITES

Serves 2 Minutes 15

Flavored popcorn

Pick your favorite flavor

You need

olive oil

½ tablespoon of unsalted butter

3 tablespoons popcorn kernels

Flavor combos

¼ cup finely grated Parmesan cheese (about ½ oz) and a few pinches of sweet smoked paprika

½ teaspoon of Marmite loosened with 1 teaspoon of boiling water

2 teaspoons maple syrup or runny honey and a few pinches of ground cinnamon or ¼ teaspoon of vanilla bean paste

1 Heat a drizzle of olive oil and the butter in a saucepan over high heat. Once melted, add the popcorn and stir well to coat.

2 Cover with a lid and let sit for a few minutes – as the popcorn starts to pop, gently shake the pan to make sure all the kernels have popped, then remove from the heat (it's ready when the popping slows down to just a few seconds apart).

3 Let cool for a few seconds, then drizzle or sprinkle on your chosen flavor combo (see below) and toss together well.

Next-level flavor

You can also supercharge your popcorn with things like balsamic vinegar or Worcestershire sauce, but to make sure it gets distributed lightly and evenly you'll need to use a spray bottle. You can usually find these in drugstores and supermarkets. Simply pour your chosen flavor into the bottle and spritz away, tossing the popcorn as you go for even coverage, then let dry. If using vinegar, just make sure you choose a thin one for easy spritzing. Have fun!

Makes 14 Minutes 20

1 per portion

No-bake oatmeal bites

Dried fruit, seeds and maple syrup

You need

4 Medjool dates

2½ cups old-fashioned rolled oats

3 tablespoons mixed seeds

½ cup mixed dried fruit

1 orange

1 tablespoon maple syrup

1 tablespoon vegetable oil

optional: 1 oz high-quality milk, dark or white chocolate, for drizzling

1 Pit the dates, if needed. Put the oats, seeds, dried fruit and dates into a food processor and blitz until nicely chopped.

2 Finely grate in the orange zest, then add the maple syrup, vegetable oil and a squeeze of orange juice. Blitz again to a soft dough.

3 Roll or press the dough out between two sheets of parchment paper to ½ to ¾ inches thick. Use a small cookie cutter to stamp out shapes (each bite should weigh around 1½ ounces). Re-form and re-roll the scraps and repeat until you've used up all the dough.

4 Place a heatproof bowl on top of a pan of lightly simmering water, break in the chocolate (if using) and stir occasionally until melted, then drizzle over the oatmeal bites and let set.

5 Pop in an airtight container – they'll keep happily for up to a week.

Serves 8 Minutes 20

Hummus and vegetable dippers

Extra-crunchy carrots, radishes, peppers, celery and cauliflower

You need

8 baby carrots

8 radishes

2 mixed-color bell peppers

4 stalks of celery

¼ of a head of cauliflower (about 8 oz)

optional: red or white wine vinegar

1 x 15-oz can of chickpeas

1 small clove of garlic

1 tablespoon tahini or peanut butter

extra virgin olive oil

1 lemon

1 Wash, trim and halve the carrots and radishes, seed the peppers and slice into strips with the celery. Break the cauliflower into bite-size florets, discarding any tough stems.

2 This is optional, but if you want to get your vegetables extra-crunchy, pop them into a bowl of cold water with lots of ice, a pinch of sea salt and a swig of vinegar 15 minutes before you want to eat them.

3 Add the chickpeas to a food processor (juices and all), and peel and add the garlic. Add the tahini or peanut butter and 1 tablespoon of extra virgin olive oil, along with a squeeze of lemon juice and a pinch of salt, then whiz until smooth, scraping down the sides of the processor bowl as needed. Have a taste and add more lemon juice, if needed, then transfer to a serving bowl.

4 Drain the vegetables (if you've soaked them) and serve alongside the hummus for dipping.

“My super-quick flatbreads (see page 140) or some toasted pitas are also great for dunking and scooping.”

Serves 1 Minutes 6

Stuffed folded tortilla

Ham, cheese, tomatoes, plus your favorite condiment

You need

1 small tortilla

1 slice of smoked ham

1 oz firm mozzarella or Cheddar cheese

1 handful of cherry tomatoes

1 teaspoon of your favorite pesto (see page 130), mustard or all-purpose tomato sauce (see page 132)

1 Place the tortilla flat on a clean work surface and make a cut from the center point downwards to the bottom edge.

2 Tear the ham over one quarter and grate the cheese over another.

3 Slice the tomatoes and arrange in another quarter, then spread the pesto, mustard or tomato sauce in the final quarter.

4 Fold up (see pages 116–117), then transfer to a non-stick frying pan over medium heat and cook for 4 to 5 minutes, or until beautifully golden, flipping halfway. Delicious served with a crunchy green salad.

Flavor switch-up

Make this veggie by simply swapping the ham for a handful of baby spinach or jarred roasted red peppers. And if you're craving a sweet treat, sliced banana, chocolate spread, toasted chopped nuts and fresh berries make an awesome combination.

Plus cooling

Banana bread

With cinnamon, honey and nuts

You need

8 tablespoons unsalted butter (1 stick), softened, plus extra for greasing

2 large eggs

4 ripe bananas

2 tablespoons runny honey

2 tablespoons unsweetened apple juice

1¾ cups self-rising flour

1 big pinch of ground cinnamon

optional: ½ cup unsalted nuts, such as walnuts, pecans, almonds or hazelnuts

1. Preheat the oven to 350°F, and lightly grease the bottom and sides of a 5 x 9-inch loaf pan.
2. Beat the butter in a mixing bowl until creamy. Crack in the eggs and beat them with the butter (if it looks lumpy, don't worry, it will fix itself).
3. Peel and mash in 3 of the bananas so you've got a mixture of smooth and chunky. Stir in the honey and apple juice, then fold in the flour and cinnamon until combined – try not to overmix.
4. Bash or roughly chop the nuts (if using), then fold them in. Spoon the mixture into the pan, then peel and slice the remaining banana and poke into the top.
5. Bake for 40 to 50 minutes, or until golden and cooked through – if you poke a skewer into the middle, it should come out clean.
6. Let the loaf cool slightly, then carefully turn out onto a wire rack to cool completely. Serve in slices – scrumptious spread with butter, nut butter, honey, jam or chocolate spread.

Helpful Hack

If you can't find self-rising flour, use an equal volume of all-purpose flour plus 1½ teaspoons of baking powder and a pinch of salt for each 1 cup of flour.

Makes 6 | Hours 1 | Minutes 15

Plus resting

Mini quiches

With cheese, vegetables and bacon

You need

1 cup all-purpose flour, plus extra for dusting

5 tablespoons unsalted butter, cold

1 small onion

1 clove of garlic

olive oil

1 handful of your favorite vegetables, such as baby spinach, mushrooms, broccoli, bell peppers, cherry tomatoes, zucchini or peas

optional: 1 slice of smoked bacon or 1 slice of smoked ham

1 large egg

scant ½ cup heavy cream

2 oz of your favorite cheese, such as Cheddar, Stilton, feta or goat cheese

1. Put the flour into a mixing bowl, cube and add the cold butter, then rub in with your fingers until the mixture resembles fine breadcrumbs. Add 2 tablespoons of cold water and mix until you get a rough dough. Bring the dough into a ball with your hands, then wrap and rest in the fridge for at least 30 minutes.
2. Peel and finely chop the onion and garlic, then add to a large non-stick frying pan over medium heat with 1 tablespoon of olive oil and cook for 5 minutes, or until soft, stirring regularly.
3. Prep your chosen vegetables – clean and slice the mushrooms, slice the broccoli into very small florets, seed and thinly slice the peppers, thinly slice the cherry tomatoes and dice the zucchini.
4. Add the vegetables to the pan (there's no need to cook the tomatoes) and cook for 3 to 4 minutes, stirring occasionally and adding splashes of water as needed. Finely chop and add the bacon or ham (if using), and season to perfection with sea salt and black pepper. Crack the egg into a liquid measuring cup, pour in the cream and beat with a fork, then grate in most of your chosen cheese.
5. Preheat the oven to 375°F. Dust a clean work surface and a rolling pin with flour and roll out the pastry so it's around ⅛ inch thick.
6. Stamp out rounds of pastry using a 4-inch pastry cutter and gently push them into the cups of a muffin tin (leftover pastry can be pressed back into a ball and re-rolled). Prick the bottom of each pastry shell with a fork.
7. Place paper liners inside each pastry shell, fill with pie weights or uncooked beans or rice, and blind bake for 15 minutes, removing the liners and weights for the last 5 minutes.
8. Divide the vegetable mixture between the pastry shells, pour in the egg mixture and grate on the rest of the cheese. Bake for 15 minutes, or until golden and just set. Delicious served hot or cold.

Serves 2-4 Minutes 15

Homemade beans on toast

With smoky paprika and grated cheese

You need

olive oil

1 cup fresh or frozen mix of diced onion, celery and carrot

½ teaspoon sweet smoked paprika

1 x 15-oz can of cannellini beans

1 x 14.5-oz can of whole tomatoes

2–4 slices of bread

unsalted butter, for spreading

Parmesan or Cheddar cheese, to serve

1. Place a large non-stick frying pan over medium heat with 1 tablespoon of olive oil, then add the vegetables and cook until softened, about 5 minutes for frozen veg and 10 minutes for fresh, stirring occasionally.

2. Add the paprika and cook for 1 minute, then pour in the beans (juices and all). Use your hands to crush in the tomatoes (or pour in and break up with a spoon as you go), then season with a pinch each of sea salt and black pepper.

3. Cook for 5 minutes, or until thickened slightly, stirring regularly.

4. Toast the bread, then divide between plates and spread lightly with butter. Spoon on the beans, and finish with a fine grating of cheese.

Serves 4 Minutes 30

Movie night veggie nachos

Corn salsa, popped beans and dressed avo

You need

6 scallions

1 long red sweet pepper

3 ripe tomatoes

optional: 1 red chili

½ cup drained canned corn kernels

optional: ½ a bunch of cilantro (about ½ oz)

2 limes

olive oil

4 whole wheat tortillas

1 x 15-oz can of black beans

1 ripe avocado

2 oz feta cheese

plain yogurt or sour cream, to serve

optional: chili sauce, to serve

1 Preheat the oven to 350°F, and place a large non-stick frying pan over high heat to heat up.

2 Trim the scallions, then put the whole pepper, tomatoes, scallions and chili (if using) into the dry pan for 10 minutes, or until soft and charred, turning occasionally. Transfer the pepper and chili to a bowl, cover and let sit for 5 minutes. Transfer the tomatoes and scallions to a board to cool.

3 Add the corn to the pan and cook for 2 minutes, then transfer to a separate bowl. Once cool enough to handle, roughly chop the tomatoes and scallions and add them to the charred corn.

4 Peel, seed and roughly chop the pepper and chili, pick and chop a few cilantro leaves (if using), then add it all to the bowl with the juice of ½ a lime, a splash of olive oil and a pinch of sea salt.

5 Pile up the tortillas and cut through the stack to make eight triangles (so you end up with 32 in total), then arrange in a single layer over two baking sheets. Bake for 15 minutes, or until golden, turning halfway.

6 Drain and rinse the beans, pat dry with paper towels, then add to the pan over medium heat and cook for 5 minutes, shaking occasionally – you want them to pop open. Peel and pit the avocado, cut into chunks, then squeeze on the juice of ½ a lime.

7 Arrange the tortilla chips on a serving platter, top with the popped beans, corn salsa and the dressed avo. Crumble on the feta, pick and sprinkle on the remaining cilantro leaves and dollop on the yogurt or sour cream and the chili sauce (if using). Cut the remaining lime into wedges for squeezing.

SKILLS
FOR LIFE

Serves 4 Minutes 15

One-cup pancakes

The simplest pancakes ever

You need

1 cup self-rising flour
(see note on page 118)

1 cup milk

1 large egg

unsalted butter or olive oil,
for frying

1 Add the flour and milk to a mixing bowl, then crack in the egg and whisk together well.

2 Place a large non-stick frying pan over medium heat with about ½ tablespoon of butter (or use olive oil), then, once melted, add large spoonfuls of batter to the pan – you'll need to cook your pancakes in batches.

3 Wait for little bubbles to form on the surface of the pancakes, about 1 to 2 minutes, then use a slotted spatula to flip them and cook for another 1 to 2 minutes, until golden on the other side.

4 Carefully wipe out the pan with a ball of paper towels, then add another ½ tablespoon of butter and cook the next batch. Serve the pancakes right away with your favorite toppings.

Top toppings

- Sliced banana, yogurt and runny honey
- Blueberries, yogurt and orange zest
- Grated apple or pear and maple syrup
- Mango or canned pineapple, yogurt, unsweetened shredded coconut and lime
- Sliced strawberries and nut butter
- Roasted rhubarb, yogurt and toasted nuts
- Crispy bacon, avocado and maple syrup or chili sauce

Pesto, three ways

Big flavor for very little effort

Green

1 small clove of garlic

1 bunch of basil (about 1 oz)

¼ cup pine nuts

2 oz Parmesan cheese

extra virgin olive oil

½ a lemon

1. Peel the garlic and place in a mortar and pestle with a pinch of sea salt.
2. Pick in the basil leaves and grind to a paste.
3. Bash in the pine nuts and finely grate in the Parmesan, then muddle in 2 tablespoons of extra virgin olive oil.
4. Squeeze in a little lemon juice to taste, and season to perfection with salt and black pepper.

Unofficial green

1 small clove of garlic

1 cup baby spinach (about 1 oz)

5 tbsp shelled unsalted pistachios

2 oz feta cheese

extra virgin olive oil

½ a lemon

1. Peel the garlic and place in a mortar and pestle with a pinch of sea salt.
2. Gradually add the spinach leaves and grind to a paste.
3. Bash in the pistachios, then muddle in the feta and 2 tablespoons of extra virgin olive oil.
4. Squeeze in a little lemon juice to taste, and season to perfection with salt and black pepper.

Red

1 small clove of garlic

¼ cup sun-dried tomatoes packed in oil

¼ cup slivered almonds

2 oz Parmesan cheese

1. Peel the garlic and place in a mortar and pestle with a pinch of sea salt.
2. Drain and add the sun-dried tomatoes, then add the almonds and grind to a coarse paste.
3. Finely grate in the Parmesan, then muddle in 2 tablespoons of oil from the tomato jar and add a splash of water to loosen, if needed.
4. Taste and season to perfection with salt and black pepper.

Makes **4** Cups

Minutes **40**

All-purpose tomato sauce

A flexible base for so many meals

You need

12 oz mixed vegetables, such as onion, leek, celery, bell peppers, carrots, zucchini and squash

2 cloves of garlic

olive oil

1 x 28-oz can of whole tomatoes

1 bunch of basil (about 1 oz)

1. Prep, peel and trim your chosen vegetables as needed, then roughly chop or coarsely grate on a box grater (or feed them through the grater attachment of a food processor to speed things up). Peel and thinly slice the garlic.
2. Drizzle 2 tablespoons of olive oil into a large saucepan over medium heat, add the garlic and fry for 1 minute, then scrape in the chopped vegetables and cook for 5 minutes, stirring occasionally.
3. Use your hands to crush in the tomatoes (or pour in and break up with a spoon as you go). Fill the can one-quarter full with water, swirl it around to pick up the last bits of tomato and pour it into the pan.
4. Simmer for 20 minutes, or until thickened slightly, tearing in the basil in the last few minutes.
5. Remove the pan from the heat and season with sea salt and black pepper – you can either serve the sauce chunky, or let it cool slightly then blitz with an immersion blender to your preferred consistency.

Big-batch favorite

You can use this handy sauce right away, cover and keep it in the fridge for up to 1 week, or divide between ziplock bags, label and freeze in portions for another day. It makes a great topping for pizzas (see page 32), is delicious tossed with pasta (see page 134) and is the perfect base for things like lasagna, chili or even soups.

Serves 4 | Minutes 15

One-ingredient pasta

Simply made with flour and water

You need

2¼ cups all-purpose or Tipo 00 flour, plus extra for dusting

1. Add the flour to a mixing bowl, then gradually mix in just enough warm water (about 10 tablespoons) to bring it together into a ball of dough – if it feels a bit sticky, add a little extra flour.
2. Knead on a lightly-floured surface for 3 minutes, or until smooth and shiny. See below for how to cut or shape your pasta.
3. Cook the pasta in boiling salted water for 2 to 3 minutes for tagliatelle or pappardelle, or 5 minutes for pici (let cook slightly longer if you've allowed the pasta to dry), then drain and toss with your chosen sauce.

For tagliatelle or pappardelle

Dust a clean work surface with flour, then use a rolling pin to roll out the pasta dough as thin as you can (aim for 1⁄16 inch), dusting it well with flour as you go – you might find it easier to work in batches. Loosely roll up the pasta sheet, then use a sharp knife to slice it just over ¼ inch wide for tagliatelle or just over ¾ inch wide for pappardelle and toss it with your hands to separate the strands.

For pici (think skinny green bean–shaped)

Simply tear off ¾-inch balls of dough, about ⅓ ounce in weight, and roll them out into long, thin sausage shapes on a clean work surface. The beauty is that they're all different, so anyone can do it.

Eggcellent pasta

If you want to see my method for fresh pasta using an egg, which has a slightly richer flavor and softer texture, see page 86.

Serves 4 Minutes 15

Perfect rice

Beautifully fluffy results every time

You need

1½ cups basmati rice

1. Pour 2½ cups of water into a saucepan, add a pinch of sea salt and bring to a boil over high heat.
2. Place the rice in a fine-mesh strainer and rinse under cold running water until the water runs clear (this will prevent the rice from sticking together as it cooks).
3. Once boiling, carefully add the rice to the water, give it a quick stir, then cover and cook over low heat for 12 minutes, or until tender.
4. Let sit for 2 minutes, then fluff up with a fork.

Bonus flavor

Once you've mastered this method, feel free to give it a flavor boost by adding extra ingredients to the water as the rice cooks – citrus zest, unsweetened shredded coconut, a bouillon cube, sun-dried tomato paste, flavored tea bags or fresh herbs or spices (cinnamon sticks, cardamom pods and turmeric all work well). Or you could simply finish with a good squeeze of lemon juice and some chopped scallions. Play around until you find your favorite combination.

Serves 4 Minutes 15

Super-quick flatbreads

Made with three simple ingredients

You need

1 ½ cups self-rising flour (see note on page 118), plus extra for dusting

½ cup plain yogurt

unsalted butter, to serve

1 Add the flour to a mixing bowl and make a well in the middle. Add the yogurt, then gradually mix together until smooth, using your hands once the dough starts to come together.

2 Dust a clean work surface and your hands with flour, then divide the dough into 4 pieces. Stretch or roll out each piece to about ¼ inch thick.

3 Put a large non-stick frying pan over medium-high heat to warm up.

4 Once hot, carefully add the dough rounds to the pan and cook for 2 to 3 minutes on each side, or until golden and puffed up – you may need to work in batches. Spread each lightly with butter and serve.

"You can eat these flatbreads simply with honey or jam, you can top them with eggs (see pages 22–25) or serve them with my vegetable curry (see page 60). I sometimes like to mix crushed garlic with a little butter, then spread it over the warm flatbreads for an epic garlic bread. Seriously tasty! You can even roll the dough into little balls instead if you prefer and cook them in the frying pan until golden – the possibilities are endless!"

Baked potatoes

Serve with your favorite toppings

You need

4 russet potatoes

olive oil

1 Preheat the oven to 375°F. Scrub the potatoes under cold running water, then pat dry.

2 Prick all over with a fork, then drizzle each potato with 1 teaspoon of olive oil, season lightly with sea salt and black pepper, then rub all over and place on a baking sheet.

3 Bake for about 1 hour (depending on how big your potatoes are), or until crispy on the outside and soft on the inside.

4 Cut the potatoes open right away – this will prevent the insides from steaming and becoming soggy.

Top toppings

- A pat of butter and your favorite grated cheese
- Homemade beans (see page 122) and grated Cheddar cheese
- Canned tuna, corn and mayonnaise
- Shake, rattle and roll rainbow salad (see page 144)
- Buddy's Bolognese (see page 48) and finely grated Parmesan cheese
- Autumn veggie chili (see page 74), sour cream and diced avocado
- Vegetable curry with cooling cucumber yogurt (see page 60)
- Sausage and bean casserole (see page 54)

Serves 8 · Minutes 20

Shake, rattle and roll rainbow salad

With mason jar dressings

You need

2 x quick mason jar dressings (see page 146)

4 small raw beets, different colors if possible (about 6 oz)

2 large carrots

¼ of a small head of red cabbage (about 6 oz)

¼ of a small head of green cabbage (about 6 oz)

2 firm pears

1 bunch of soft herbs, such as mint, chives, Italian parsley or tarragon (about 1 oz)

1¼ cups shelled walnuts or pecans

Fantastic leftovers

This salad is delicious rolled up in a wrap with a grating of cheese or shredded roast chicken – great for a picnic or packed lunch, just pack the salad elements separately and quickly assemble just before digging in.

1. Make your chosen dressings – you can stick with one type or serve up a mixture.
2. Scrub the beets and carrots under cold running water, then trim and halve them. Trim away the cabbage core, cut into quarters, then core the pears and slice into quarters, discarding the stems.
3. Put the coarse grater attachment into a food processor and push through all the vegetables in the following order (so the red cabbage and beets are at the bottom of the processor bowl and the juice doesn't stain everything else): red cabbage, beets, carrots, green cabbage and finally the pears, or use a box grater to do this by hand.
4. Turn the contents of the bowl out onto a large serving platter so you get piles of rainbow colors.
5. Pick and finely chop the herb leaves and place in a small bowl, then crumble the nuts (bash first if easier) into another small bowl.
6. Serve the platter, herbs, nuts and dressings in the middle of the table so that everyone can make and dress their own salad – just remember you can always add more dressing but you can't take it away.

Each makes 8 Tablespoons

Minutes 5

Quick mason jar dressings

Lemon, yogurt or strawberry and balsamic

Lemon

1 lemon

6 tablespoons extra virgin olive oil

1 tablespoon runny honey

1. Squeeze the lemon juice into a lidded glass jar, add the extra virgin olive oil and the honey, then season with a pinch each of sea salt and black pepper.
2. Put the lid on the jar and shake well.

Yogurt

5 tablespoons plain yogurt

2 tablespoons white or red wine vinegar

1 tablespoon extra virgin olive oil

1 sprig of Italian parsley

1 sprig of mint

1. Put the yogurt, vinegar and extra virgin olive oil into a lidded glass jar.
2. Pick and finely chop the herb leaves, then add to the jar with a pinch each of sea salt and black pepper.
3. Put the lid on the jar and shake well.

Strawberry and balsamic

6 ripe strawberries

6 tablespoons extra virgin olive oil

2 tablespoons balsamic vinegar

1. Coarsely grate the strawberries, then place in a lidded glass jar.
2. Add the extra virgin olive oil and balsamic vinegar, then season with a pinch each of sea salt and black pepper.
3. Put the lid on the jar and shake well.

SWEET TREATS

Serves 6 Minutes 15

Choccy microwave mug cake

With bananas or raspberries

You need

3½ oz dark chocolate (70%)

7 tablespoons unsalted butter, cold

2 tablespoons runny honey

2 bananas or scant 2 cups raspberries

2 medium eggs

½ cup self-rising flour (see note on page 118)

2 oz high-quality milk or white chocolate

optional: 6 tablespoons plain yogurt

"Me and my sister Petal make these almost every week for a quick chocolaty treat."

1. Break the dark chocolate into a large microwave-safe mixing bowl. Cube and add the butter, then drizzle in the honey.
2. Microwave in 30-second bursts on medium heat, stirring each time, until the chocolate has completely melted.
3. Peel and mash 1 banana, or mash half the raspberries, and add to the chocolate mixture. Crack in the eggs, beat with a fork, then fold in the flour.
4. Divide the mixture between 6 small microwave-safe mugs or cups.
5. Break the milk or white chocolate into chunks and push them into the mixture, then microwave in two batches on high for 1½ minutes, or until risen and slightly gooey in the middle.
6. Slice the remaining banana and divide between the mugs, or simply dot with the remaining raspberries, and serve with a dollop of yogurt (if using).

Makes 16 Minutes 30
Plus cooling

Ginger nut cookies

With a touch of cinnamon

You need

¾ cup self-rising flour (see note on page 118)

1 teaspoon baking soda

1½ teaspoons ground ginger

½ teaspoon ground cinnamon

¼ cup packed light brown sugar

4 tablespoons unsalted butter (½ a stick)

2 tablespoons golden syrup or honey

1 Preheat the oven to 325°F and line two large baking sheets with parchment paper.

2 Add the flour, baking soda, ginger, cinnamon and sugar to a mixing bowl and stir well. Melt the butter with the syrup or honey in a small saucepan, then pour into the bowl and mix to a soft dough.

3 Divide the dough into 16 portions and roll each piece into a ball. Arrange on the prepared sheets, leaving space between them, then press down to flatten slightly.

4 Bake for 12 minutes, or until beautifully golden and starting to crack. Let cool on the sheets for 10 minutes, then transfer to a wire rack to cool completely.

Serves 6 Minutes 20

Grilled fruit salad

Finished with lime and mint

You need

½ a pineapple

½ a cantaloupe

3 ripe kiwis

2 cups strawberries

1 ½ cups seedless grapes

1 lime

½ a bunch of mint (about ½ oz)

coconut or plain yogurt, to serve

1 Soak 12 wooden skewers in cold water to prevent them from burning later on, and preheat your grill or grill pan.

2 Peel and core the pineapple, peel and seed the melon, then chop them both into generous 1-inch chunks. Peel and quarter the kiwis, and trim the tops off the strawberries, halving any larger ones. Pick the grapes off the stems. Gently thread the fruit onto the skewers.

3 Carefully transfer them to the grill or grill pan and cook for 2 or 3 minutes on each side, then slide the fruit off the skewers into a serving bowl or onto a platter – you may need to work in batches.

4 Squeeze on the lime juice, tear and sprinkle on the mint leaves, and toss it all together. Serve with the yogurt for dipping or dolloping.

Helpful hack

If you're finding that some of your fruit is wobbly on the skewer, use the grapes to secure the ends, as they sit nice and tightly on the skewer.

Serves 18 Minutes 45

Plus cooling

Party sheet cake

With fresh berries and sprinkles

You need

16 tablespoons unsalted butter (2 sticks), softened, plus extra for greasing

1 cup plus 2 tablespoons granulated sugar

4 large eggs

1⅔ cups self-rising flour (see note on page 118)

1 heaping teaspoon baking powder

1 teaspoon vanilla bean paste

Buttercream and topping

10 tablespoons unsalted butter, softened

1 teaspoon vanilla bean paste

1¾ cups confectioners' sugar

2 tablespoons naturally colored sprinkles

1 Preheat the oven to 325°F, then lightly grease a 9 x 13-inch baking pan and line it with a sheet of damp parchment paper.

2 In a food processor, blitz the butter and sugar together until light and fluffy (or you can beat it by hand). One by one, crack in the eggs, then add the flour, baking powder and vanilla bean paste, and keep blitzing until smooth.

3 Spoon the mixture into the prepared pan and spread out evenly. Bake for 25 minutes, or until golden and risen – if you poke a skewer into the middle, it should come out clean. Cool a little in the pan, then transfer to a wire rack to cool completely.

4 To make the buttercream, cut the butter into cubes, then beat with the vanilla bean paste for 2 minutes, or until creamy (save yourself a bit of time by using a stand mixer, if you have one).

5 Sift the confectioners' sugar into a mixing bowl, then gradually add it to the butter a few spoonfuls at a time. Once all the sugar has been incorporated, beat for another 4 to 5 minutes, or until pale and fluffy.

6 Add a small splash of water to the buttercream and fold in to loosen slightly, if needed, then spread over the top of the cake, using a spatula to smooth out and spread it right to the edges.

7 Top with the sprinkles, then serve as is or decorate with things like berries, chocolate shavings and lots of candles. Enjoy!

13.
BUDDY!

Serves **12** Hours **1** Minutes **45**

Plus cooling

Totally tropical pavlova

With passion fruit, kiwis, bananas and coconut

You need

4 large eggs

1 cup superfine sugar

1 lime

1 cup Greek yogurt

4 ripe kiwis

2 bananas

2 passion fruits

1 tablespoon unsweetened shredded coconut

optional: 1 sprig of mint

1. Preheat the oven to 250°F, and line a large baking sheet with parchment paper.
2. Separate the eggs, placing the whites in a large clean mixing bowl (save the yolks for another recipe). Using a hand mixer or a stand mixer, beat the egg whites on high until they form stiff peaks – you'll know the meringue is thick enough if you can tip the bowl upside down over your head and it doesn't fall out.
3. While still whisking, gradually add the sugar and a pinch of sea salt. Beat for another 4 to 5 minutes, or until opaque and glossy. Dip a clean finger into the mix and rub against your thumb – if the mixture feels grainy, keep beating for another 2 minutes.
4. Dot a tiny bit of meringue on each corner of the parchment, then flip it over and press down – this will secure it to the pan. Dollop the meringue onto the parchment and spread it out into a 10-inch round, using the back of a spoon to create little wispy bits on the top.
5. Bake for 1 hour and 15 minutes, or until crisp on the outside and chewy in the middle, then turn off the oven and let the meringue cool in the oven.
6. When you're ready to assemble, finely grate the lime zest and mix with the yogurt. Carefully peel and slice the kiwis (a mixture of rounds and half-moon shapes looks nice), peel and slice the bananas, then squeeze on the lime juice and gently toss together.
7. Transfer the meringue to a serving plate. Spoon the yogurt onto the meringue and smooth it out. Arrange the kiwis and bananas nicely on top, then cut the passion fruits in half and spoon on the flesh. Sprinkle with the coconut, then pick, chop and sprinkle on the mint (if using).

Serves 6 Minutes 5

Quick fruity froyo

Yogurt, lime and runny honey

You need

1 lb of your favorite frozen fruit, such as raspberries, blueberries, blackberries, mangoes or bananas

generous 2 cups plain yogurt

1 lime

optional: 2 sprigs of mint

runny honey, to taste

1. Place the frozen fruit (you can stick to one type, or choose your favorite combination) in a blender with the yogurt.
2. Finely grate in the lime zest and squeeze in all the juice. Pick in the mint leaves (if using).
3. Blitz until smooth, then have a taste and sweeten with a little honey, if needed.
4. Spoon into bowls and serve right away, or if you want to be able to scoop it and/or serve it in ice cream cones, pop it into the freezer for 2 hours before serving.

Helpful hack

If serving in bowls or tumblers, pop them into the freezer to get nice and cold before you start – this will prevent the froyo from melting too quickly.

Serves 6 | Hours 1 | Minutes 10

Apple and berry crumble

With a nutty oaty topping

You need

4 apples

1 lb fresh or frozen berries

½ an orange

8 tablespoons unsalted butter (1 stick)

1 cup all-purpose flour

scant ⅓ cup hazelnuts

⅓ cup rolled oats

generous ⅓ cup demerara or turbinado sugar

1. Preheat the oven to 350°F. Peel and core the apples, chop into 1-inch chunks, then place in an 8 x 8-inch baking pan.
2. Scatter in the berries, finely grate in the orange zest and squeeze in the juice, then mix well.
3. Cube the butter, then add to a mixing bowl with the flour and rub together with your fingertips until the mixture resembles fine breadcrumbs.
4. Bash or roughly chop the hazelnuts, then add to the bowl along with the oats and sugar. Mix well, then sprinkle evenly over the fruit.
5. Bake for 45 minutes, or until golden and cooked through. Delicious served with custard, yogurt or ice cream.

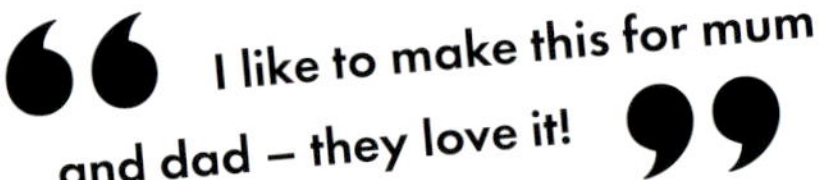

Serves 16 Minutes 20

Plus chilling

Rocky road

With white chocolate drizzle

You need

olive oil, for greasing

4 oz dark chocolate (70%)

4 oz high-quality milk chocolate

8 tablespoons unsalted butter (1 stick)

¼ cup golden syrup or honey

8 large marshmallows (or 1 cup mini marshmallows)

5 oz cookies, such as ginger nuts (see page 154), digestives or Biscoff (about 20 small cookies)

scant ¾ cup unsalted nuts, such as pistachios or toasted hazelnuts

3 oz chocolate-covered honeycomb (like Crunchie bars, or you could use malted chocolate balls)

¼ cup glacé cherries or dried fruit

2 oz high-quality white chocolate

1 Lightly grease a 9 x 13-inch baking dish and line it with a sheet of damp parchment paper.

2 Place a heatproof bowl on top of a pan of lightly simmering water, break in the dark and milk chocolates, add the butter and syrup or honey, and stir occasionally until melted.

3 Quarter the marshmallows (keep mini marshmallows whole), break up the cookies, roughly chop or bash up the nuts, bash up the honeycomb and halve the cherries or dried fruit, if needed, then stir them into the chocolate mixture.

4 Pour into the prepared dish and chill in the fridge for at least 4 hours, then carefully turn out.

5 Break the white chocolate into a clean heatproof bowl and melt as described in step 2 (or melt in the microwave, if easier). Drizzle the melted chocolate over the rocky road, let set in the fridge, then cut up and serve.

Make it festive

Transfer the mixture to a 4-cup greased and lined pudding mold or bowl before chilling, then turn it out, pour on melted white chocolate and decorate with artificial holly to turn it into a Christmas pudding (see page 170).

Helpful kitchen notes

Choose good ingredients

Using high-quality ingredients in your cooking makes a big difference. When you're shopping, always look at what's available, pick and choose carefully, and if there are different levels of quality, buy the very best you can afford. When it comes to meat, fish, seafood and eggs, try to choose seasonally and responsibly, and look out for higher-welfare options.

Welcome seasonality

These days we can get almost everything all year round, but buying seasonally means that there are always new ingredients to look forward to. If you learn to shop for fruit and vegetables when they're in season, you will benefit hugely – it's not just about the nutritional and flavor benefits, it will often save you money, too.

Wash fruits and vegetables

Remember to give everything a good wash before you start cooking, especially if you're using it raw.

Handle food safely

Cooking food at the right temperature will ensure that any harmful bacteria is killed. When cooking burgers, sausages, chicken and pork, cut into the middle to check that it's no longer pink, that any juices run clear, and that it's piping hot. It's safe to serve steak pink in the middle as long as it's been properly sealed to kill any bacteria on the meat's surface. Once meat, chicken or fish are cooked, lift them out of the pan and serve them using clean utensils that haven't touched the raw food.

Organize your pantry

When you want to cook, the pantry is an exciting place to start. It's a good idea to organize your spices, oils, vinegars, condiments and so on in separate areas to use the space efficiently. It's also a good idea to stock up on staples that have a long shelf life, like rice, pasta, and dried and canned goods.

Freezing and defrosting

Remember to let food cool thoroughly before freezing, and get it into the freezer within 2 hours. Make sure everything is well wrapped, and labeled for future reference. Thaw in the fridge before use, and use within 48 hours. If you've frozen cooked food, don't freeze it again after reheating or defrosting it.

Manage your fridge

Being smart about how you organize your fridge will make it easier for you not to waste food. Keep any vegetables in the crisper drawer so that they stay nice and fresh. Make sure any cooked foods or leftovers are covered, and any uncooked meat and fish are well wrapped and put on the bottom shelf to prevent them from contaminating anything on the other shelves. Put any food that's ready to eat, whether it's cooked or doesn't need to be cooked, on a higher shelf, away from the raw meat or fish. It's also a good idea to rotate newer and older food so that you use them in the right order.

A bit about oven temperatures

All recipes are tested in fan ovens in °C and then converted to °F for this book – find conversions for conventional and gas ovens online.

Useful kitchen tools

Here's a list of basic kitchen equipment that'll help you make the recipes in this book, and beyond! Please don't worry if you don't have everything – just use what you've got available.

- [ ] Cutting board
- [ ] Knives
- [ ] Kitchen scale
- [ ] Measuring cups (liquid and dry)
- [ ] Measuring spoons
- [ ] Mixing bowls
- [ ] Vegetable peeler
- [ ] Box grater
- [ ] Fine grater or Microplane
- [ ] Rolling pin
- [ ] Whisk
- [ ] Wooden spoon
- [ ] Slotted spoon
- [ ] Rubber or silicone spatula
- [ ] Slotted spatula
- [ ] Tongs
- [ ] Colander
- [ ] Fine-mesh strainer
- [ ] Potato masher
- [ ] Can opener
- [ ] Paper towels
- [ ] Parchment paper
- [ ] Aluminum foil
- [ ] Saucepans
- [ ] Non-stick frying pans
- [ ] Dutch oven
- [ ] Roasting pans
- [ ] Baking sheets
- [ ] Baking dishes
- [ ] 12-cup muffin tin
- [ ] Loaf pan

Nice to have

- [ ] Food processor
- [ ] Blender
- [ ] Toastie maker or panini press
- [ ] Stand mixer
- [ ] Mortar and pestle

Knife skills for kids

Having good knife skills can make you more efficient in the kitchen, but you need to take care when using these tools so you don't get hurt. It's important to keep focused on what you're doing, and remember, practice makes perfect!

Here are some handy techniques that you can use to help you on your journey to good knife skills.

How to hold a knife safely

Place your thumb and forefinger around the base of the blade in a pinching position, then wrap the remaining three fingers around the handle of the knife. Your index finger and thumb should be opposite each other, on either side of the blade, with the remaining three fingers loosely curled around the handle.

The bridge

Use the bridge technique to cut ingredients into smaller, more manageable pieces.

Form a "bridge" over the ingredient with your hand, making sure the arch is nice and high so there's plenty of room for the knife to fit underneath. Hold the item securely with your fingers on one side and your thumb on the other, then pick up the knife with the other hand and position the blade under the bridge. Cut into the ingredient, pressing the knife firmly into the middle and sliding it back towards you out of your bridge. Once you've halved the ingredient, place it flat-side down and cut into smaller pieces, if needed.

The claw

Use the claw technique to slice ingredients into thinner strips.

Place the ingredient on the board, flat-side down. Make a "claw" by curling your fingers closely together over the ingredient, tucking them under so you can't see your fingertips. Pick up the knife with your other hand – the flat side of the blade actually rests against the first knuckle of the claw, protecting the fingers. Keeping the tip of the knife on the board, slice through the ingredient, sliding the knife forwards as you cut and then back. Repeat, ensuring you have a good grip and keeping your fingers together at all times.

The bridge

The claw

Rock chopping

This technique uses a rocking motion to chop, combined with the claw to keep your fingers safe.

Hold the knife firmly in one hand and place the tip of the knife on the board at an angle of roughly 45 degrees. With the other hand, make a "claw" over the ingredient, tucking your fingertips out of the way. Using the curve of the knife, push down and forwards in a rocking motion – the tip of the knife doesn't leave the board. Move your claw back before making each slice. Practice makes perfect: don't go too fast! The side of the knife blade should rest against the first knuckle of the guiding hand, helping keep the blade perpendicular to the cutting board. To make your next slice, move your fingers back along the item, keeping your fingers together and keeping a firm grip on the top.

Cross chopping

Cross chopping is used to cut ingredients into much smaller pieces – for example, fresh herbs.

Hold the knife firmly in one hand, place the tip of the knife on the board at an angle of roughly 20 degrees. Keep the fingers of your other hand rigid on the top edge of the lower half of the blade. Keeping the tip of the knife on the board, raise and lower the handle of the knife, like a guillotine, so it chops whatever is under it. Gather back the ingredients into the middle and continue to cross chop until you have the size you want.

Safety checklist

- ✓ Secure your cutting board
- ✓ Never wave a knife in the air
- ✓ Keep the handle clean for a good grip
- ✓ Chop ingredients flat-side down whenever possible
- ✓ Slice small pieces off round ingredients to create a flat, stable surface
- ✓ Don't chop too quickly
- ✓ Clean your knife safely
- ✓ Keep your knife sharp
- ✓ Always hold a knife in your dominant hand
- ✓ Practice makes perfect!

Rock chopping

Cross chopping

10 TIPS TO LIVE HEALTHILY AND HAPPILY

My dad's Nutrition Team helped me to make sure that the recipes in this book are the right balance between nutritious everyday foods and things to be enjoyed occasionally. The recipes can be enjoyed by your whole family, so just dish up smaller portions if you're cooking for little brothers or sisters. They've also got some handy tips on a good approach to building positive eating habits that are easy to remember and will help you on the path to leading a healthier, happier life.

1. Always eat breakfast!

Kick-start your day in the right way with a nutritious, balanced breakfast so you can rebuild your energy levels after hours of being asleep.

Did you know? Studies have shown that young people who eat breakfast have better memory and concentration skills.

2. Balance and variety are key

Eat from all five food groups to get the wide range of nutrients your body needs. The picture of the Eat Well Guide (see page 180) is a really clear way to see the balance you should be aiming for. Try to eat a balance throughout the week and you'll be in great shape.

3. Eat the rainbow!

This is a fun one – eating all different colors of vegetables and fruits is important because they each contain different vitamins and minerals that all play a part in keeping us healthy.

Challenge: Try to eat at least five 80g/3-oz portions (or 40–60g/1½-2-oz portions for younger children) of vegetables and fruit a day – you can choose from raw, frozen, canned or cooked!

Did you know? Dried fruit (30g/1 oz), fruit juice and smoothies (150ml/5 oz), beans and legumes (80g/3 oz) can each only count as one portion of our 5-a-day.

4. Upgrade your carbohydrates

Carbohydrates are found in foods like bread, rice and pasta, and provide the main fuel for our bodies. When you can, try switching to whole wheat and whole grain varieties, like whole wheat bread and brown rice. They help us feel fuller for longer, and provide more vitamins, minerals and fiber than white carbohydrates.

Eat well guide

It's all about balance

5. Mix up your proteins

You'll find protein in things like beans, fish, eggs, meat, nuts and tofu. Try to include different kinds of proteins in your meals. Think of proteinas the building blocks of our bodies – it's used for growth and repair, and is important for healthy muscles and bones.

6. Include dairy

Add dairy, such as milk, cheese and yogurt, to your meals – it's packed full of important nutrients, especially calcium for strong bones and healthy teeth. Non-dairy alternatives, like plant-based drinks, should have key nutrients added to them (look for calcium, iodine and vitamin B12 on the label to make sure).

7. Choose healthy fats

Unsaturated sources of fat, such as olive, vegetable and canola oils, as well as nuts, seeds, avocado and rich oily fish are healthiest for us. They provide us with essential fatty acids and help us absorb vitamins and nutrients from foods.

8. Know your sugars

Sugar is found naturally in things like milk and dairy products (lactose) and whole fruits and vegetables (fructose) and that's okay. It's great to include these foods as part of a balanced diet. Free sugars, which are added to foods and drinks, and those that are found in honey, syrups and juices, are best enjoyed occasionally, not all the time.

9. Season to taste

Taste your food before you add salt, as you may not need to add any. And seasoning with herbs and spices can be equally, if not even more, delicious – give it a try! Although we do need a small amount of salt, having too much isn't healthy for us.

10. Stay hydrated

Drink plenty – it's an essential part of life! Water, reduced-fat milk, and sugar-free drinks count. Juices and smoothies also count, but only one small glass per day.

Challenge: Try to drink six to eight glasses of water per day.

NEVER GIVE UP

THANK YOU

Thanks so much to everyone who has helped and supported me on this amazing project – it's been SO much fun, and I'm really proud of how it turned out. Special thanks to Mum and Dad, and to Poppy, Daisy, Petal and River, as well as the Cooking Buddies gang. You're the best!

And big thanks to the rest of the team:

David Loftus
Paul Stuart
Richard Bowyer

Beth Stroud
Rebecca Verity

James Verity
Davina Mistry

Ginny Rolfe
Isla Murray
Holly Cowgill
Maddie Rix
Maggie Musmar

Jenny Rosborough
Rozzie Batchelar
Lucinda Cobb

Tamsyn Zietsman
Lydia Waller
Rosalind Godber
Ashleigh Bishop
Letitia Becher
Richard Herd

Kevin Styles
Louise Holland
Zoe Collins

Louise Moore
Ione Walder
Dan Hurst
Elizabeth Smith
Clare Parker
Tom Troughton
Ella Watkins
Juliette Butler
Lee Motley
Nick Lowndes

Christina Ellicott
Anjali Nathani
Joanna Whitehead
Stuart Anderson
Annie Lee
Jill Cole
Emma Horton
Catherine Hookway

Sean Moxhay
Samantha Beddoes
Anna Stickland
Mark Drake
Alice Binks
Gurvinder Singh
Anita Goundar
Josh Javed
Jon Padovani
Amanda Doig-Moore
Renzo Luzardo

Index

Recipes marked V are suitable for vegetarians; in some instances you'll need to swap in a vegetarian alternative to cheese such as Parmesan.

C

Q

R

S

T

For more inspiration:

bbc.co.uk/food
bbc.co.uk/iplayer
jamieoliver.com
youtube.com/cookingbuddies

First published in the UK by Penguin Michael Joseph,
part of the Penguin Random House group of companies.

Published in Canada by Appetite by Random House®,
a division of Penguin Random House Canada Limited
320 Front Street West, Suite 1400
Toronto, Ontario, M5V 3B6, Canada

Library and Archives Canada Cataloguing in Publication is available upon request.
ISBN: 978-0-525-61337-4
eBook ISBN: 978-0-525-61338-1

Recipe and portrait photography by David Loftus
Cover portrait & additional photography by Paul Stuart (pages 4, 9 & 191)
Design by Jamie Oliver Limited
Color reproduction by Altaimage Ltd

Printed in China

The authorized representative in the EU for product safety and compliance is
Penguin Random House Ireland, Morrison Chambers, 32 Nassau Street,
Dublin D02 YH68, Ireland, https://eu-contact.penguin.ie

penguinrandomhouse.ca

First Canadian Edition

10 9 8 7 6 5 4 3 2 1

Penguin
Random House
Canada

Penguin Random House is committed to a sustainable future for our business, our readers and our planet. This book is made from Forest Stewardship Council® certified paper.